AMERICAN NURSES ASSOCIATION

MODEL

PRACTICE

ACT

If you are interested in purchasing updates to this document, please send your name, address and fax number to:

Winifred Y. Carson, Esq.
Nursing Practice Counsel
American Nurses Association
600 Maryland Ave., SW, Suite 100 West
Washington, DC 20024

Published by
American Nurses Publishing
600 Maryland Avenue, SW, Suite 100 West
Washington, DC 20024-2571

ISBN 1-55810-128-4

NP- 110   .5M   5/96

TABLE OF CONTENTS

ACKNOWLEDGMENTS

This document was developed under the direction of the ANA Congress of Nursing Practice, chaired by Linda R. Cronenwett, PhD, RN, FAAN (1990-1994), and Mary K. Walker, PhD, RN, FAAN (1994-1996), with input from the Ad Hoc Committee on Credentialing in Advanced Practice, Beverly Malone, PhD, RN, FAAN, chair, and the Institute of Constituent Members on Nursing Practice Executive Committee, Carole Alexander, MS, RN, chair.

The Congress of Nursing Practice extends special thanks to Judith E. Haber, PhD, RN, CS, FAAN, Gail A. Harkness, DrPH, RN, FAAN, and Maureen E. Shekleton, DNSc, RN, FAAN, for serving as the review committee for the Congress of Nursing Practice. The Congress of Nursing Practice and staff also thank Barbara J. Safriet, JD, LLM, assistant dean, Yale College of Law, and Karen A. Ballard, MA, RN, New York State Nurses Association, for their review and assistance with the development of the ANA Model Practice Act.

Special thanks to Winifred Y. Carson, Esq., Nursing Practice Counsel, for research, development and ongoing support in the completion of this project.

Congress of Nursing Practice, 1994-1996
  Mary K. Walker, PhD, RN, FAAN, *Chair*
  Katreen R. Collette, MS, RN
  Jo A. Franklin, MS, RN, CNA
  Judith E. Haber, PhD, RN, CS, FAAN
  Gail Harkness, DrPH, RN, FAAN
  Christine M. Kinavy, MS, RN
  Mary S. Koithan, MSN, RN
  Fang-Lan Wang Kuo, EdD, RN
  Frank P. Lamendola, MSN, RN, CS
  Tona L. Leiker, MS, RN, ARNP, CARN
  Karen S. Martin, MSN, RN, FAAN
  Judith L. Martin-Holland, MS, MPA, RN
  Kathleen M. Poi, MS, RN, CNAA
  Maureen E. Shekleton, DNSc, RN, FAAN
  Susan Tullai-McGuiness, RN, MPA
  Julie M. Wooden, RN,C, CERN

Congress of Nursing Practice, 1990-1994
  Elizabeth O. Dietz, EdD, RN, CS
  Darlene Johnson, MA, RN, CNA
  Nancy Savage, PhD, RN

ANA Department of Practice and Office of General Counsel
  Karen S. O'Connor, MSN, RN, former Deputy Director for Policy and Programs
  Sarah Stanley, MSN, RN, Director, Department of Practice
  Winifred Y. Carson, Esq., Nursing Practice Counsel
  Eunice Turner, MSN, RN,C, Senior Policy Analyst
  Sandra Yamane, Legislative Analyst
  Russell Moss, Esq., Law Clerk
  Linda J. Minich, Senior Administrative Assistant
  Yvette Cook, Administrative Assistant

INTRODUCTION

In 1994, the American Nurses Association (ANA) House of Delegates requested that ANA staff draft an innovative state nursing practice act to reflect changes in the practice environment, including provisions reflecting ANA policy. Responding to the rapid changes facing nursing practice, state nurses associations (SNAs) had expressed a need for such model legislation and, thus, the ANA Model Practice Act was born.

The ANA Model Practice Act includes a guide and commentary to explain the changes being proposed. Unlike previous ANA state legislative models, this model will be subject to annual review and change in structure and provisions to ensure that it incorporates new legal decisions and precedents related to state licensure laws. Further, ANA will use this model to initiate discussion of changes in the regulation of nursing practice and provide legislative drafting options for members.

The ANA Model Practice Act also incorporates innovative approaches which are designed to withstand legal review and challenge. This model has not been structured to emulate any state's practice act. Instead, staff review and professional consultation have been used to model a draft responsive to nursing needs based on existing provisions in state practice acts which have been successful, and incorporate these with new language to address anti-competitive barriers to practice.

There has been little written on the regulation of nursing practice. Aside from two articles by Barbara Safriet, JD, LLM, SJD, few legal scholars have studied the structure of regulatory and administrative legal limitations on the licensure of nursing practice. Against this background, ANA's Ad Hoc Committee on Certification in Advanced Practice[A] reviewed a 1992 ANA staff compilation of state practice acts, other state statutes, and regulations associated with advanced practice to determine the impact existing law has on the recognition and acknowledgment of advanced practice. This survey looked at various aspects of practice acts and regulations to determine whether the nurse in advanced practice was regulated through licensure, certification, registration, or alternative forms of regulation. The resulting report also addressed some of the speculation and colloquial beliefs about advanced practice. Among other findings in the 1992 report were:

• **There is a limited connection between reimbursement and statutory recognition of advanced practice.** Advocates of second licensure contend that reimbursement occurs with statutory recognition or licensure of advanced practice, although surveys of state laws indicate otherwise.[1]

• **Boards of Medicine (BOMs) are unduly involved in the regulation of nursing practice.** There are 24 states with some form of joint regulation, with some states allowing physicians and others to intervene into the actions of the Board of Nursing (BON) and assist or define the scope, tasks, and educational levels of advanced practice nurses (APNs).[2]

[A] The Ad Hoc Committee on Certification in Advanced Practice was renamed the Blue Ribbon Panel on Advanced Practice in 1994. The American Nurses Association has published Model Practice Acts for a number of years, including 1976, 1978, 1980, 1981, and 1990.

• **The scope of practice of the nurse in advanced practice is not defined consistently from state to state.** Over 40 different titles are used in the regulation of advanced practice and virtually every state has its own unique definition of advanced practice.[3]

• **States are gradually changing their advanced practice laws and regulations to incorporate the clinical nurse specialist (CNS) in the advanced practice statutes.** Thirty-five states have been identified as including the regulation of clinical nurse specialists as APNs in their statutes or regulations.[4]

• **Nurse-midwives and nurse anesthetists, if not covered by the advanced practice statute, have been effective in obtaining recognition in those states where nurses in advanced practice are recognized.**

• **Inconsistencies of note in advanced practice law and regulation include:**
    - failure to include title protection/title recognition.
    - few specific causes of action related to scope/responsibilities of the nurse in advanced practice.
    - lack of advanced practice membership on BONs.

Additional barriers to advanced practice have been identified through ANA staff review and assessment of state nursing practice acts. The October 1994 Congress on Nursing Practice (CNP) "Report on Model Legislation for Nurse Practice Acts: A Status Report" listed these barriers as:

• **Disciplinary process.** The disciplinary sections of existing practice acts are not comprehensive and do not cover all activities/known deficiencies in nursing practice. Specifically, the disciplinary structure is not designed to address advanced practice nursing scopes of practice. Since nurses do not control administrative decisions to utilize unlicensed personnel, the use of the discipline process to address delegation problems inappropriately targets and sanctions nurses.

• **BON composition.** Statutes dedicate seats to specific specialties or classes of nurses without considering the demographics of the licensed nursing population. Instead of periodic review and adjustment of board compositions, seats are added as groups request representation.

• **BON regulatory responsibilities.** By focusing solely on discipline and licensure, BONs tend to avoid the larger issue of institutional infringements on nursing practice. Boards continue to work within traditional boundaries for regulating practice, without looking at newer approaches to regulation such as sanctions created in law to address activities by other entities which may adversely affect nursing practice. State Boards seldom use hospital, insurance, or consumer protection laws to address the inappropriate provision of nursing care. And, by ignoring existing practice setting structures, Boards all too often inappropriately use their existing power only to sanction nurses who cannot control the work setting or staff utilized.

• **Prescriptive authority as an added privilege or part of the scope of nursing practice.** As legislation and regulations related to advanced practice nursing evolved, nurses settled for treating prescriptive authority and other advanced practice functions as additions to the scope of nursing practice instead of expansions of the traditional boundaries of nursing practice. This approach created the foundation for the ongoing debate and fractionalization of registered and advanced nursing practice.

• **Reciprocity or endorsement**. With the inconsistencies in the regulation of advanced and specialty practice nurses, it is hard for nurses to move from one jurisdiction to another. Moreover, advanced practice and specialty nurses are unable to retain a core of expanded skills given the differences among state nurse practice acts.

• **Structure of grandparenting provisions**. Another barrier created by the approach taken to developing advanced practice law compelled states to create differing and inconsistent grandfather provisions which impede the easy transfer of title and authority from one jurisdiction to another.

• **Title recognition or title protection**. Because states use myriad different titles and few states limit use of the term to those authorized to practice, consumers are confused and often mistakenly use inappropriate or inconsistent titles. Often, health care facilities, though knowledgeable about nurse titling, deliberately title unlicensed staff in a manner akin to advanced and specialty practitioners, thus promoting inappropriate use of non-nursing staff and misleading the public which believes non-nurses are nursing staff.

The CNP's report discussed other issues relevant to advanced practice nursing including reimbursement and mandatory malpractice requirements, collaboration provisions and their benefits or drawbacks vis-à-vis advanced practice nurses, registered nurse (RN)/licensed practical nurse (LPN) scope and requirements, and dual licensure of nurses.

ANA MODEL PRACTICE ACT: DISCUSSION OF MAJOR PROVISIONS

Primacy Theory for Regulating Professions

Nurses continually face impediments when defining the scope of their practice. These impediments--cultural, legal and professional--are based upon the constitutional characteristics and inconsistencies of the United States' licensure system. In large part, nurses continue to fight a battle which ended almost a century ago, when various states adopted all-encompassing medical practice acts. With these statutes, physicians received an official monopoly to treat illness and control the practice rights of other health care providers.[B] This monopoly on practice has structured virtually every aspect of the regulation of licensure of health professionals. Using the licensing practices associated with medicine as a barometer, state legislators have supported the status quo in the face of nurses and other health professionals fighting to expand nursing practice.

As is the case for other health professionals, the scope of nursing practice originally evolved only with the acceptance or acquiescence of medicine to changes in practice. However, nurses continually encounter barriers to competition created by the all-encompassing scope in medical practice acts. With the advent of APNs and a move by the profession to obtain statutory recognition, physicians used their political clout to exert a strong influence on the scope of advanced practice, resulting in the development of requirements which impede utilization of nurses to the full scope of their practice.

Examples include:

- redefining collaboration as supervision, thus requiring physician participation in every aspect of patient care.

- inconsistencies in the public reimbursement rates for RN and physician's assistant (PA) practice, which creates economic incentives to use PA providers; and, further, by compelling private-insurer retention of reimbursement rates and procedures which favor physician use.

- use of accreditation regulations to limit the scope of APNs, for example, by limiting the ability of nurses to supervise and control inpatient, institutional care.

- retention of control over the nurse privileging process.

- continued use of PRN and physician orders to compel independence of practice by RNs while retaining control over payments for services, rates, and charges.

[B] Safriet, B. J. 1994. Impediments to Progress in health care workforce policy: License and practice laws. *Inquiry* 31: 310-317; Freidson, E. 1970. *Professional dominance: The social structure of medical care.* New York: Atherton Press; Rayack, E. 1983. Medical licensure: Social costs and social benefits. *Law and Human Behavior* 7: 147-156.

The pervasiveness of medicine, combined with nursing's response to existing regulatory domination, have affected the entire structure of nursing practice acts and the evolution of the profession. In addition to limitations on advanced practice, specialty nursing which formerly went unregulated now must have statutory recognition to receive reimbursement. Some states now regulate the relationship between RNs and APNs to the point of determining whether APNs can regulate RN practice.

Nursing must change its paradigm. Instead of retaining the presumption of medical supremacy over all health care practices, nursing must accept Dr. Safriet's challenges and rethink its approach to the regulation of nursing practice by changing the basic presumptions of licensure.

The ANA Model Practice Act includes provisions to describe the role of the BON in the regulation of nursing practice (Section 3). A contemporary proponent of the primary legal right of professions to regulate themselves, Safriet cites examples where nurses have ceded their authority to regulate nursing practice, such as in instances where nursing and medical practices overlap. Consistent with this theory, the ANA Model Practice Act includes a mandate for the profession to regulate and define the boundaries of practice and provide nurses with the tools to challenge medical infringement upon the defining of non-medical practice.

Expansion of Model Practice Act

Previous ANA model legislation only regulated registered nurse practice. However, the new Model Practice Act regulates licensed practical/vocational nurses (LP/VNs), registered nurses (RNs) and advanced practice registered nurses (APRNs) under one statute. Approximately 20 states currently regulate LP/VNs and RNs under the same statute. Additionally, numerous states which regulate LP/VNs and RNs also regulate nursing assistants, medical technicians, and other typically unlicensed personnel. Consistent with ANA's members' desire for an accurate reflection of existing regulatory models, this Act was written to include LP/VNs and provide the Board with the authority to regulate every aspect of nursing practice.

Unlicensed Personnel

Likewise, though it does not contain language applying to unlicensed personnel, the ANA Model Practice Act does include provisions which allow the Board to develop a system for training and regulating all persons who provide nursing care.[c] As nursing continued to debate the regulation and use

---

[c] These sections mandate that nurses ascertain and enforce reasonable and uniform standards for delegation of nursing functions to include, if Boards deem appropriate the education and training of personnel who will be responsible for delegating or fulfilling the task to be delegated. Further, the "Disciplinary Causes of Action" section specifically prohibits willful practice with (an) unlicensed or unauthorized person(s) or aiding such unlicensed or unauthorized person(s) to practice nursing in a manner inconsistent with Board regulations.

The "Disciplinary Causes of Action" section also includes prohibitions against knowingly delegating a nursing function, task, or responsibility to (an) unlicensed or unauthorized person(s) when the delegation involves substantial risk of harm to a patient or client, and prohibits any person (conducting nursing functions) from performing or offering

of unlicensed personnel, the ANA Model Practice Act was drafted to include strong provisions to protect the scope of nursing practice. These provisions allow the BON to:

- develop standards for appropriate delegation of nursing functions.

- sanction those unlicensed persons who provide nursing care.

- sanction nurses who inappropriately delegate nursing tasks or work with persons who are not appropriately trained to provide nursing care.

- enjoin every aspect of illegal nursing practice regardless of licensure status.

Advanced Practice

Implicit in virtually every nurse practice act is the presumption that advanced practice should be regulated separately from licensed or practical nursing practice. Upon review of the first, original amendments authorizing advanced practice, ANA staff found most states emulated one another and addressed advanced nursing practice by adding on provisions instead of restructuring the practice act. This approach of legislating additions to the practice act, solely for advanced practice nurses, fostered debate around defining advanced practice and lobbying for development of second licensure to create a new category of regulation for advanced practice.

Scopes, however, read differently, because legislators subject to pressure from various organizations and professional groups inserted language into the practice act which was often inconsistent with how advanced practice nurses functioned in the work setting. The limitations (i.e., direct supervision, mandated collaboration, prescriptive authority requiring co-signature on nursing prescriptions, or supervision of prescribing through collaborations or protocol or use of a physician-developed formulary) create a dichotomy between practice and regulation. Consistent with ANA policy that nurses should be regulated under a common scope of nursing practice, the ANA Model Practice Act was written to include advanced practice under the definition of nursing practice, thus allowing the BON to make professional distinctions in tasks by levels of practice.

Unlike any state practice act, the definition of nursing in the Model Practice Act includes some tasks that are clearly at the practical/vocational, registered professional, and advanced nursing practice levels. This provision (Sec. 2), combined with the authority of the Board (see Sec. 4(B)(1)), allows the Board, through ruling, to make differentiations in practice consistent with present educational levels without amendment of the practice act every time the scope of nursing practice changes (see also Sec. 2(H)). Further, as additional specialties emerge, whether registered or advanced practice nursing (see Sec. 12(B)), the BON may again specify appropriate educational and professional certification requirements.

---

or attempting to perform services beyond the scope of those authorized by the practice act or regulations.

Few educational and professional certification requirements for medical specialties are incorporated in statute; if articulated, they are included in the board's regulations. Consequently, we can use the Safriet theory of constitutional interpretation to design and structure the Model Practice Act. To ensure the effectiveness of this change, nursing should conduct discussions about defining scope--though not levels of practice--legislatively, to ensure that all within the nursing community understand and appreciate the expansiveness of including advanced practice within the scope of all registered nursing practice. This expansiveness and flexibility allows the profession--not the BON--to define the practice. Flexibility allows nursing educators to re-tool and restructure programs to reflect health care delivery needs and not the requirements of licensure and, if necessary, to redesign the requirements for each level of practice. Flexibility also promotes nursing experimentation with various models of health care delivery.

Certification of Schools of Nursing

Nursing is the only profession which has retained authority to certify educational curriculum for the profession through the licensure board. This certification process has given rise to the use of differing educational standards to evaluate schools of nursing. Many states use the National League for Nursing (NLN) certification process; others opt for alternative certifications, with some Boards individualizing the certification process to address specific state need. This structure reinforces inconsistencies in nurse educational levels.

Within nursing, organizations have challenged the ability of the profession to develop a uniform educational base for licensure. Externally, national organizations reviewing trends in workplace structure, health care delivery, and licensure have challenged the structure of the regulation of all licensed professions and noted the administrative burden placed on states which allow licensure categories to regulate each profession differently.

ANA believes the profession should regulate education. Variances in state licensure models related to educational certification do not enhance efforts being made to standardize nursing educational models and competencies. The ANA Model Practice Act removes the authority from the Board to certify schools of nursing. Instead, ANA recommends that professional nursing organizations and associations support one or more organizations conducting the certification process. ANA also supports development of standardized curriculum for every level of nursing practice.

To address the secondary concerns associated with the loss of revenue from removal of the certification approval process, the ANA Model Practice Act incorporates provisions authorizing the Board to develop and enforce reasonable and uniform standards for delegation of nursing functions.

Board Composition and Responsibilities

Although the Board responsibility for the certification of schools of nursing has been removed, the overall responsibility of the Board has been expanded. Section 3 expands the scope of licensure and regulation of nursing practice by allowing the Board to define nursing practice and Section 4 provides for omnibus rule-making authority where the Board is responsible for not only implementing the ANA Model Practice Act as drafted, but also:

1. interpreting and enforcing the scope of nursing practice through advisory and board opinions;

2. adopting regulations necessary to implement the Model Act, including defining the scope of each level of nursing practice and authorizing the practice of APRNs;

3. developing and enforcing reasonable and uniform standards for delegation of nursing functions;

4. developing and enforcing reasonable and uniform standards for all levels of nursing practice;

5. issuing subpoenas, examining witnesses, and administering oaths;

6. investigating complaints of alleged violations of the Act;

7. receiving and reviewing complaints of violations of the Act and regulations issued pursuant to the Act;

8. conducting hearings and keeping records and minutes necessary to carry out Board functions;

9. invoking, or requesting that the State invoke, disciplinary action against a licensee or an unauthorized person practicing nursing;

10. issuing advisory opinions on nursing practice;

11. determining nursing professional and related multidisciplinary group structure appropriate for independent nursing practice as professional or limited liability corporations; and,

12. examination, licensure, and renewal of the licenses of qualified applicants.

While many of these provisions are optional[D] , they are listed in the Model Practice Act to provide direction in drafting legislation. In states which require statutes that specifically list Board functions, this list also can be used.

Additional authority has been granted to the Board under the ANA Model Practice Act to address the need for nurses to be among those professions permitted to develop limited liability or professional corporations. Limited liability and profession corporations are the preferred organizational structures

---

[D] Those that are included in the brackets under Section 4 of the Act are optional.

for managed care entities. However, this corporate structure tends to limit by statute the type of professional who can organize this type of corporation.

Many states are using the Uniform Limited Liability Corporations Act to develop or amend statutes regulating the formation of limited liability corporations. That act gives authority to the licensing authority to make determinations of structure or types of provider included in these organizations. By giving the Board the authority to make these determinations, the ANA Model Practice Act provides nursing with an option to remove the statutory barriers to creation of professional nursing or multidisciplinary corporations.

Provisions dedicating seats on the Board to any specific nursing category have been removed from the ANA Model Practice Act. This change was incorporated to allow flexibility in Board composition, to enhance diversity in Board membership, and to allow new specialties to compete for Board nomination without requiring amendment of the law. The Board, if it deems appropriate, may make designations through regulations.

Some Boards tend to consider professional membership ethically inconsistent with Board membership. Again, nursing is the only profession to place this restriction on licensure Board nomination or membership. Sec. 5 includes provisions to ensure that professional membership is not considered an ethical conflict, which requires removal from the Board. Sec. 5 also includes an optional provision to include newly licensed nurses on the Board. This provision is offered to compel nursing to rethink its policy of including only "seasoned" professionals on the Board and to support mentoring of new nurses, helping them better understand the Board process. This provision expands the breadth of knowledge of the Board by including newly licensed nurses who can explain new nursing techniques and educational processes.

Causes of Action

The Model Practice Act's list of disciplinary causes of action, expansive as it may seem, was taken from existing nursing practice acts. The list includes virtually every type of cause of action that may be applicable to the practice of nursing. Some Boards contend they do not have adequate authority to initiate administrative discipline for some nursing as well as non-nursing activities. Using this list of causes of action provides existing legal precedent for the application of some causes of action which may not exist under a particular nursing practice act. Thus, if they are challenged, one can refer to the law of the state where the cause of action is presently being used. While another state's law does not have the weight of the jurisdiction's law, it can provide the court with clear precedent of how the law can be used.

Additional causes of action have been created in the Model Practice Act to address existing deficiencies in nursing practice acts. Attention was given to developing causes of action to regulate APRNs. Also, causes of action were refined to address inappropriate delegation of nursing practice.
ANA has concerns about state Boards of nursing using the limited licensure provision to regulate persons with disabilities. Originally, limited licensure status has been given to those persons who are

being disciplined and require additional BON supervision and oversight. A disabled person may not need further direction. This provision has been expanded in state laws to provide states with options through which they can regulate the practice of disabled nurses. State laws are being structured to require applicants to complete a self-assessment tool, which includes questions about one's history of substance abuse and one's mental or physical condition, to determine if the nurse can comply with the essential job requirements of a RN.

Boards of nursing are creating lists of "essential" job functions and other screening documents. ANA has serious concerns about the legality of these lists and the use of this approach. By using this category of licensure to make distinctions between disabled persons who may be able to provide nursing services under certain circumstances and/or with reasonable accommodation, the BON brings attention to that individual, and may unwittingly provide a basis for employment discrimination, without subjecting the employer to the requirements of the ADA. The ADA did not provide licensure boards with exemptions to assist or promote discrimination against licensees.

ANA also is concerned about the eligibility screening requirements for nurses and their relationship to the essential job functions. The Department of Justice (DOJ) has reviewed licensure board questions to ascertain whether some of the questions violate the ADA[E] . This review required DOJ to look at why certain questions were asked and how they were posed. Cognizant of each state licensure board's responsibility to protect the health and safety of the public, DOJ noted:

> "Generally, a public entity is prohibited from applying eligibility criteria that screen out or tend to screen out individuals with disabilities from fully and equally enjoying any service, program, or activity. A public entity may, however, impose neutral rules and criteria that screen out or tend to screen out, individuals with disabilities if the criteria are necessary for the provision of the service, program, or activity being offered.... This provision of the Department's regulation prohibits attempts by state or local governments to identify unnecessarily the existence of a disability."

Given this opinion and the case law, ANA believes that Board eligibility requirements are problematic if used to screen individuals during the licensure process and that the criteria used to evaluate essential nursing are subjective and overly broad. It is ANA's contention that if the eligibility requirements are used to evaluate ability to function, nurses presently providing services and care consistent with the scope of their position description will be screened out unnecessarily and inappropriately labeled through the imposition of limited licensure status.

Nursing is not only a physical process, but also a sophisticated, cognitive one. The dimensions of nursing care extend from RNs who provide direct patient care to the nurse administrator who directs, manages, and coordinates nursing services. The physical and intellectual requirements of the profession vary greatly. Nursing jobs also vary greatly. Nurses may provide direct patient care through hospitals

---

[E] U.S. Department of Justice, Civil Rights Division, Public Access Section letter of April 6, 1993, to the Assistant Director for Licensure and Administration of the Arizona Board of Medical Examiners (DJ 202-PL-213).

and other acute care facilities or within the home environment. Or nurses may provide services through analytical or research-based processes.

The use of physical, intellectual, and mental health criteria could limit or otherwise condition the license of a person already practicing registered nursing. The application of these criteria may not address the subjective nature of nursing jobs and responsibilities. Further, this limitation may be inappropriate and inconsistent with the intent of the ADA.

Eligibility requirements do not reflect a substantial relationship between the required functions and the statutory scope of nursing practice, nor are they supported by nursing data which accurately reflect essential requirements for registered nursing practice. While ANA respects the authority of Boards to fulfill their role as regulators, it believes any document requiring substantial interpretation of state law which could change the licensure status of those presently practicing nursing requires formal administrative rule making. This process mandates that boards provide reasons for regulation and background information in a government-published document that is available to all interested parties for review and comment during a specified period.

Prescriptive Authority

The ability to prescribe is included in the nursing scope of practice (Section 2(I)), with authority to regulate the practice vested in the BON under Section 4(B). Consistent with ANA policy on advanced practice scope and regulation, the authority to regulate the practice is vested in the BON. Thus, the Board may:

- presume prescribing drugs, therapies, and devices is implicit in advanced nursing practice and incorporate prescriptive authority in its certification of advanced practice, or

- set up a second level of requirements and create additional certifications.

Based on ANA's position that all advanced practice functions should be included within the scope of nursing practice, the ANA Model Practice Act places the responsibility for regulating prescriptive practice under the regulation of the Board. Through regulations, the BON may define the appropriate scope and levels for prescriptive practice. And these changes should now remove the artificial barriers to nurse prescribing.

Anti-Competitive Limitations

Sec. 21 of the Model Practice Act is fashioned after language included in the District of Columbia Health-Care and Community Residence Facility, Hospice and Home Care Licensure Act of 1983, which specifically prohibits discrimination against nurse-midwives and nurse practitioners in the privileging process. It has been expanded to include provisions to protect nurses from every aspect of anti-competitive behavior and incorporates state antitrust law into the Model Practice Act by reference.

Although the District of Columbia Health-Care and Community Residence Facility, Hospice and Home Care Licensure Act of 1983 has been on the books, it has not been used to challenge nurse privileging practices as being overly expansive or exceeding the intended reach of antitrust protections. Moreover, this law has been structured to address anti-competitive practices which affect registered nursing practice and may well address some of the anti-competitive practices occurring within managed-care delivery systems.

Certification versus Regulation

The term regulation covers several different concepts related to public and professional regulation. States can and do use a number of modes of occupational regulation other than licensure. Some are spin-offs of the basic regulatory forms and can include the use of practice standards with registration or certification. Some states have developed regulatory schemes which include:

- practice standards (without special enforcement);
- practice standards (with special enforcement);
- regulation through supervision by an already licensed practitioner;
- enforcement or strengthening of existing statutes relating to deceptive or unfair trade practices;
- assignment of inspection or other supervisory authority to an existing agency; or,
- licensure of home care agencies, nursing homes, or hospices, instead of the individual.

There are two types of regulation--public and private. Private regulation arises from the desire of members of a particular profession to ensure standards, values, and safe practices. Private regulation occurs in voluntary settings, with members of the profession using informal networks to define the essence of the livelihood. When the authority is the profession, the regulation is private/professional, voluntary, and internal--i.e., occurs within the profession.

Public regulation is conducted by the government. Licensure is based on the authority of the state to protect its citizens under the police authority vested in the state by the U.S. Constitution. Additionally, the federal government has a general authority to regulate matters related to health. When the authority is vested in the government, regulation is public, mandatory, and external--i.e., occurs outside the profession.

Nursing is at an impasse: the profession desires continued utilization of private certification to assure competency, while Boards question the role of professional certifying organizations participating in the regulatory process. Although legal challenges to professional participation are virtually nonexistent, regulatory organizations are seeking alternatives to address concerns related to the diversity in educational curricula and degree requirements for RNs and APNs.

ANA believes that professional certifying organizations bring substantial knowledge and expertise to the regulatory process and recommends that nursing regulatory organizations look beyond their immediate vantage points to assess how a unilateral removal of all other certification organizations from the testing and licensure process will be perceived by the public, and assess the benefits as well as the disadvantages that will result from using one regulatory organization to certify nursing practice. Likewise, the role of nursing specialty associations should be reviewed to determine whether they can be expanded to assist Boards in their regulatory functions.

Conclusion

ANA offers its Model Practice Act to provide all SNAs with model legislation that can be used and adapted to suit their individual needs. The ANA Model Practice Act will provide SNAs with workable options and appropriate narrative to make positive decisions on the structuring of their states' nurse practice acts. This model is not designed to be used line for line, but, instead, in selected pieces, with provisions lifted and incorporated into existing state practice acts as necessary.

DRAFT LEGISLATION

A BILL

to regulate the practice of nursing.

BE IT ENACTED, BY THE _____ , that this Act be cited as the _____Nursing Practice Act.

SUBCHAPTER I. NURSING; DEFINITIONS; SCOPE

SEC. 2. GENERAL DEFINITIONS.

(A) "Act" means the Nursing Practice Act.

(B) "Advanced Practice Registered Nurse" means a registered professional nurse who has specialized knowledge, education and skills to provide health care as determined appropriate by the Board of Nursing through administrative rule making and by fulfillment of all qualifications outlined in this Act. They are registered professional nurses with national certification as deemed appropriate by the Board of Nursing, and include nurse practitioners, nurse anesthetists, nurse-midwives and clinical nurse specialists.

(C) "Assistive Personnel" means those persons who provide health care or who are used to assist in the provision of nursing care without licensure and/or with or without certification as recognized by the state.

(D) "Board" means the Board of Nursing.

(E) "Health care occupation" means a health care practice that is regulated through licensure, certification or other means by the state.

(F) "Health care professional" means a person licensed under state law to practice a health care occupation.

(G) "Licensed practical/vocational nurse" means an individual who has knowledge, education and skills to provide practical or vocational nursing care as determined appropriate by the Board of Nursing through administrative rule making and by fulfillment of all qualifications outlined in this Act.

(H) "Licensing authority" means the entity which makes determinations related to professional licensure as discussed in the state model professional corporation laws **[citation needed]** means the Board of Nursing.

(I) "Nursing" means the performance of any acts to care for the health of the patient that require substantial, specialized or general knowledge, judgment and skill based upon principles of the biological, physical, behavioral and social sciences as defined through rules promulgated by the Board of Nursing. Skills which may be utilized in the performance of this profession include:

(1) observing, assessing and recording of physiological, behavioral and social signs and symptoms of health, disease and injury, including the performance of examinations and testing and their evaluation;

(2) providing family assessment, discharge planning, therapeutic, preventive and restorative nursing care and services;

(3) counseling and educating patients about the promotion of health, prevention of disease, illness and injury and promotion of peaceful death;

(4) administering, supervising, delegating and evaluating nursing services;

(5) teaching nursing;

(6) executing nursing and medical regimens consistent with the education and clinical expertise of the registered nurse;

(7) performing acts of nursing and medical diagnosis and prescribing nursing and medical therapeutic, corrective measures and devices;

(8) performing other acts consistent with the education and training recognized by the nursing profession as properly performed by licensed/vocational, registered and advanced practice nurses; and,

(9) conducting research relevant to nursing practice.

The Board of Nursing shall determine the skill level and scope of practice for each type of nurse licensed under this Act.

(J) "Person" means an individual, corporation, trustee, receiver, guardian, representative, firm, partnership, society, school or other entity.

(K) "Registered professional nurse" is an individual who has knowledge, education and skills to provide registered professional nursing care as determined appropriate by the Board of Nursing through administrative rule making and by fulfillment of all qualifications outlined in this Act.

SEC. 3. SCOPE OF ACT

(A) This Act shall cover all aspects of licensure and regulation of nursing practice including the practice of advanced practice registered nurses as determined appropriate by the Board.

(B) This Act does not limit the right of an individual to practice nursing or any other licensed health care profession that he or she is authorized to practice under this Act or any other state licensure law.

(C) The practice of any health care occupation regulated by the state is expansive, with each licensing board vested with the responsibility to articulate and enforce the scope of each respective profession.

(D) The Board has the primary responsibility for interpreting and enforcing the scope of nursing practice through regulations and advisory and board opinions.

SUBCHAPTER II. ESTABLISHMENT OF BOARD OF NURSING; MEMBERSHIP; TERMS

SEC. 4. ESTABLISHMENT; DUTIES

(A) There is established a Board which shall be responsible for the implementation and enforcement of this Act. The Board shall be composed of ____ members. ____ members shall be nurses, and ____ shall be consumer members.

(B) The duties and powers of the Board shall include:

(1) adopting regulations necessary to implement this Act, including regulations to define the scope for each level of nursing practice and to authorize the practice of advanced practice registered professional nurses;

(2) administering and enforcing this Act and regulations and opinions issued pursuant to this Act related to nursing practice;

(3) examination, licensure and renewal of the licenses of qualified applicants;

(4) ascertaining and enforcing reasonable and uniform standards for delegation of nursing functions;

(5) enforcing reasonable and uniform standards for all levels of nursing practice;

(6) issuing subpoenas, examining witnesses and administering oaths;

(7) investigating complaints of alleged violations of this Act;

(8) receiving and reviewing complaints of violations of this Act and regulations issued pursuant to this Act;

(9) conducting hearings and keeping records and minutes necessary to carry out Board functions;

(10) invoking, or requesting that the State invoke, disciplinary action against a licensee or an unauthorized person practicing nursing;

(11) issuing advisory opinions on nursing practice; and,

(12) determining nursing professional and related multidisciplinary group structure appropriate for independent nursing practice as professional or limited liability corporations.

SEC. 5. QUALIFICATIONS OF MEMBERS

(A) Each member of the Board shall be a resident of the State at the time of appointment and remain a resident during his or her tenure on the Board.

(B) Each professional member of the Board, in addition to the residency requirements articulated in subsection (A) of this section, shall have been engaged in the practice of registered professional or licensed practical vocational nursing for at least ___ years preceding appointment. At least one member of the Board shall have become licensed within 5 years preceding appointment.

(C) Membership activity or holding an elected or appointed position in any professional organization shall not be a bar to appointment to or service on the Board.

(D) Each consumer member of the Board, in addition to the residency requirements of subsection (A) of this section, shall:

(1) not be a health care professional or in training to become a health care professional; and,

(2) Not own, operate or be employed in a business which has as its primary purpose the sale of goods or services to health care professionals or health care facilities.

[The Governor or Board shall have the right to override these requirements for consumer members if the consumer discloses any and all conflicts of interest, as articulated under this section, and agrees not to vote on any matter in which he or she or one's business or concern may benefit financially from the decision.]

(E) Each professional member of the Board shall disqualify himself or herself from:

(1) acting on his or her own application for licensure or license renewal; or,

(2) any matter related to his or her own practice of nursing.

[The Board shall have the option of allowing professional members to disclose conflicts and, upon agreement of a majority of the Board, without the affected party voting, consent to the professional member's participation based on disclosure of the conflict.]

SEC. 6. TERMS OF MEMBERS; FILLING OF VACANCIES

(A) Terms of office shall be ____ years.

(B) Of the members initially appointed under this Act, ____ shall be appointed for a term of 2 years, ____ shall be appointed for a term of 3 years, and ____ shall be appointed for a term of 4 years. The terms of the members of the Board, after the initial terms, shall expire on the fourth anniversary of the date when the first members, constituting a quorum, took the oath of office.

(C) At the end of each term, a member shall continue to serve until a successor is appointed and sworn into office.

(D) A vacancy on the Board shall be filled in the same manner as the original appointment was made.

(E) A member appointed to fill a vacancy shall serve only until the expiration of the term or until a successor is appointed and sworn into office.

SEC. 7. LIMITATION ON CONSECUTIVE TERMS

No member of the Board shall be appointed to serve more than ___ full-time consecutive terms.

SEC. 8. REMOVAL

(A) The Governor of the State or the Board may remove a member of the Board for incompetence, misconduct, conflict of interest or neglect of duty after due notice and opportunity for a hearing.

(B) The Board shall be responsible for defining the standards for removal through regulation.

SUBCHAPTER III. LICENSURE OF REGISTERED PROFESSIONAL NURSES AND LICENSED PRACTICAL/VOCATIONAL NURSES

SEC. 9. LICENSE REQUIRED

A license is required to practice nursing.

SEC. 10. EXEMPTIONS

(A) The provisions of this Act prohibiting the practice of nursing without a license shall not apply to an individual:

(1) who administers treatment or provides advice in any case of emergency;

(2) employed in the State, the District of Columbia or a territory of the United States by the federal government, while he or she is acting in the official discharge of the duties related to federal employment, provided the employing agency has a mandated licensure provision for registered professional or licensed practical/vocational nurse practice, and the employee retains a current license to practice within one of the fifty states, the District of Columbia or the territories of the United States;

(3) licensed to practice nursing in another state who is called to [state] in professional consultation by or on behalf of a specific patient to visit, examine, treat or advise the specific patient or to give a demonstration or clinic, provided that the individual engages in the consultation, demonstration or clinic in affiliation with a comparable nurse licensed pursuant to this Act, provided the trips are sporadic and the affiliation does not exceed 6 months, except upon review by and receipt of permission from the Board to extend the period of consultation, treatment or demonstration;

(4) licensed to practice nursing in another state who is traveling with a specific patient through the state, provided that the individual who travels with the patient has made arrangements to ensure continuity of care to the patient upon arrival at the destination of the patient;

(5) licensed to practice nursing in any adjoining state who treats patients within [state] if:

(a) the nurse does not have an office or other regularly appointed place within the state to meet patients;

(b) the nurse registers with the Board of Nursing and pays a fee as determined by the Board prior to practicing in the state;

(c) the state in which the nurse is licensed allows nurses licensed by [your state] to practice in that state under reasonable conditions set forth in its Nurse Practice Act, licensure or other relevant statutes; and

(d) the period of practice does not exceed 6 months, except upon review by and receipt of permission from the Board to extend the period of consultation, treatment or demonstration.

(6) enrolled in a recognized school or college as a candidate for a degree or certificate in nursing, graduate studies related to nursing practice or some form of advanced registered nursing

practice, or enrolled in a recognized postgraduate training program provided that the practice is performed:

(a) as a part of the individual's course of instruction, or as a postgraduate prerequisite for licensure;

(b) under the supervision of a nurse who is either licensed to practice in the state or qualified as a teacher of the practice of nursing by the Board;

(c) at a hospital, nursing home or health care facility operated by the state or federal government, a health care education center or other health care facility considered appropriate by the school or college; and,

(d) in accordance with procedures established by the Board.

(7) An individual who does not hold himself or herself out as a nurse, by title, description or services, or otherwise, shall not be considered to be practicing nursing as regulated by this Act.

(8) Nothing in this subsection shall be construed as exempting any of the following from other applicable laws and regulations of the state or federal government:

(a) any minister, priest, rabbi, officer or agent of any religious body or any practitioner of any religious belief engaged in prayer or any other religious practice or nursing practice solely in accordance with the religious tenets of any church for the purpose of fostering the physical, mental or spiritual well-being of any person; or,

(b) any person assisting in the care or peaceful death of a friend or member of the family, including the administration of remedies or medications, or care of the sick by family, companions or volunteers.

(9) Notwithstanding the provisions of this section, unlicensed persons who provide nursing care and do not comply with this Act shall be cited for practicing nursing without a license and may be sanctioned in a manner consistent with Subchapter IV of this Act.

SEC . 11. GENERAL QUALIFICATIONS OF APPLICANTS

(A) An individual applying for a license under this Act shall establish to the satisfaction of the Board that that individual:

(1) has not been convicted of an offense which bears directly on the fitness of the individual to be licensed;

(2) has completed the minimal educational program, required under this Act, in registered nursing at a school approved through regulation by the Board or another state Board of Nursing with standards substantially equivalent to the standards of **[state]**.

> (a) Licensed practical/vocational nurses are required to have completed a prescribed course in practical/vocational nursing at a school accredited nationally and with such accreditation as determined appropriate by the Board.

> (b) Registered professional nurses are required to have completed a course of study in registered nursing and received a degree at a school accredited nationally or with accreditation as determined appropriate by the Board.

> (c) Advanced practice registered nurses are required to have completed a master's degree in nursing or a related area of specialized knowledge as determined appropriate by the Board.

(3) has passed an examination administered by the Board given pursuant to regulations promulgated by the Board to practice nursing; and,

(4) meets any other requirements established by the Board and established by regulation to assure that the applicant has the proper education, expertise, experience and qualifications to practice nursing.

(B) The Board shall promulgate additional regulations to acknowledge certification of advanced practice registered nurses.

(C) The Board may deny a license to an applicant whose license to practice a health care occupation was revoked or suspended in another state if the basis of the license revocation or suspension would have caused a similar result in **[state]**, or if the applicant is the subject of pending disciplinary action regarding his or her right to practice in another state.

(D) The Board may grant limited licensure to nurses with disabilities pursuant to Section 23 of this Act.

SEC. 12. APPLICATION FOR A LICENSE

(A) An applicant for a license shall:

> (1) submit the required application to the Board; and,

> (2) pay the applicable fees established by the Board.

(B) The Board may establish a fee schedule for additional charges, to include:

(1) late charges;

(2) charges for certification;

(3) fees for licensure by reciprocity or endorsement;

(4) fees for reactivation of inactive licenses;

(5) special charges for limited licensure status; and,

(6) any additional reasonable charges for services provided by the Board.

(C) The Board shall publish a fee schedule as rule making in a manner consistent with the appropriate state Administrative Procedures Act **[citation needed]**.

SEC. 13. ISSUANCE OF LICENSE

The Board shall issue a license to an applicant who meets the requirements of this Act and any applicable regulations issued pursuant to this Act.

SEC. 14. RECIPROCITY AND ENDORSEMENT

(A) The Board, in its discretion, may issue a license through reciprocity or endorsement to any applicant:

(1) who is licensed as a nurse or certified as an advanced practice registered nurse and in good standing under the laws of another state with requirements which, in the opinion of the Board, were substantially equivalent at the time of licensure to the requirements of this Act and which admit health care professions licensed by **[state]** in a like manner, pursuant to an agreement with the licensing state.

(B) The Board, in its discretion, may also accept the certification of an advanced practice registered nurse if there is compliance with subsection (A) of this section, and the state licenses, certifies or recognizes advanced practice registered nurses or their equivalent.

(C) The Board, in its discretion, may issue a license to an applicant who is currently licensed or certified and is in good standing under the laws of this or any other state which has standards for licensure comparable to the requirements of Subchapter III or Section 32 of this Act.

SEC. 15. REQUIREMENTS FOR PRACTICE

(A) An individual who fails to renew a license to practice nursing shall be considered unlicensed and subject to the penalties outlined in this Act or regulations promulgated under the Act if that individual continues to practice nursing.

(B) Upon application by the licensee and payment of a status fee, the Board shall place a license on inactive status. While on inactive status, the individual shall not practice or offer to practice nursing.

SEC. 16. REINSTATEMENT OF EXPIRED, INACTIVE LICENSES

(A) If an individual fails or chooses not to renew his or her nursing license, the Board shall reinstate the license only if the individual:

(1) pays the fee established by the Board;

(2) complies with the current requirements for renewal of license; and,

(3) pays the established fee, as promulgated by the Board, for reactivation or renewal of a license.

(B) The Board shall not reinstate the license of a nurse who fails to apply for reinstatement of a lapsed or expired license within 5 years of the license expiration date. The individual may become licensed by meeting the requirements for initial licensure.

SEC. 17. TERM AND RENEWAL OF LICENSES

A license term runs ___ years from the date of issuance or renewal unless the Board, by regulation, changes the expiration date or the period of licensure.

SEC. 18. CONTINUING COMPETENCY

The Board may establish by regulation any continuing competency requirements as condition for renewal of licenses under this Act.

SUBCHAPTER IV. REVOCATION, SUSPENSION OR DENIAL OF LICENSE OR PRIVILEGE; LIMITATIONS ON LICENSURE

SEC. 19. DISCIPLINARY CAUSES OF ACTION

(A) The Board, subject to the right of hearing as provided by this Act, on an affirmative vote of a majority of its members, may take one or more of the disciplinary actions provided in this Act against any applicant, licensee or any person permitted by this Act to practice nursing who:

(1) violates any provision of this Act or regulations issued pursuant to this Act;

(2) fraudulently or deceptively obtains, attempts to obtain or uses a nursing license;

(3) is disciplined by a licensing or disciplinary authority or convicted or disciplined by a court

of any jurisdiction for conduct that would be grounds for disciplinary action under this section;

(4) has been convicted in any jurisdiction of any crime involving moral turpitude, if the offense bears directly on the fitness of the nurse;

(5) abuses any narcotic or controlled substance, and has neither requested nor received treatment for the drug addiction or abuse;

(6) provides or attempts to provide professional services while under the influence of alcohol or while using any narcotic or controlled substance or any other drug in excess of therapeutic amounts or without medical indication, and has neither requested nor received treatment for drug addiction or abuse;

(7) willfully makes or files a false report or record in the practice of nursing;

(8) willfully fails to file or record any medical report as required by law, impedes or obstructs the filing or recording of the report or induces another to fail to file or record the report;

(9) on proper request in accordance with law, fails to provide details of a patient's medical record to a health care provider or another health care professional licensed under state law;

(10) willfully makes a misrepresentation in treatment;

(11) willfully practices nursing with an unlicensed or unauthorized person or aids an unlicensed or unauthorized person in the practice of nursing in a manner inconsistent with Board regulations;

(12) knowingly delegates a nursing function, task or responsibility to an unlicensed or unauthorized person when the delegation involves substantial risk of harm to a patient or client;

(13) submits false statements to collect fees for unprovided services or submits statements to collect fees for services which are not a documented necessity;

(14) violates state and federal laws regulating drugs, including inappropriate prescribing, dispensing or administering practices;

(15) performs or offers or attempts to perform services beyond the scope of those authorized by this Act or regulations promulgated pursuant to this Act;

(16) fails to report facts known regarding incompetent, unprofessional, unethical or illegal practices of a health care professional or health care provider, unless the individual knows or reasonably believes that such facts have already been reported and disciplinary actions have been taken by the appropriate health care licensing board;

(17) fails to pay a civil fine imposed by the Board, administrative officer or court;

(18) willfully breaches a statutory, common law, regulatory or ethical requirement of confidentiality with respect to a person who is a patient or client of the registered nurse, unless ordered by the court;

(19) discriminates against a patient or client based on race, gender, sexual preference or orientation, ethnicity, economic status or disease state/illness or in the provision of services;

(20) performs professional services under unsanitary conditions;

(21) engages in sexual harassment of a colleague, patient or client;

(22) physically or verbally abuses a colleague, patient or client;

(23) fails to use sufficient knowledge, skills or nursing judgment in the practice of nursing as defined by the level of licensure;

(24) assumes duties and responsibilities on repeated occasions, without sufficient preparation or for which competency has not been achieved or maintained;

(25) exploits the patient or client for financial gain or offers, gives, solicits or receives fees for referral of a patient or client; or,

(26) violates an order of the Board or violates a consent decree of or negotiated settlement entered into with the Board.

SEC. 20. OTHER UNLAWFUL ACTS

(A) The practice of nursing for compensation by a person, corporation or other business entity who is not licensed, or whose license is suspended, revoked or expired is declared to be in violation of state law and shall constitute a public nuisance, which shall be actionable under state civil law **[title and citation needed]** or this Act.

(B) Notwithstanding the provisions of state law, any action taken to prohibit nurses from practicing in a manner consistent with this Act, including any limitations on clinical privileging, reimbursement, prescribing drugs or performing other activities-- consistent with state and national standards of nursing practice as deemed appropriate by the Board through regulation--which impose economic restraints or limitations on nursing practice shall be prohibited.

(C) Nothing in this section shall prohibit or penalize compliance with federal laws applicable to nursing practice.

SEC. 21. SANCTIONS AVAILABLE

(A) Upon determination by the Board that an applicant, licensee or other individual has committed any of the acts prohibited in Section 20 of this subchapter or any other section of this Act, the Board may:

(1) deny a license to an applicant;

(2) revoke or suspend the license of any licensee;

(3) rcvokc or suspend the privilege to practice in [statc] permitted under this Act;

(4) reprimand any nurse permitted by this Act to practice in [state];

(5) impose a civil fine not to exceed $_____ for each infraction by any applicant, licensee or nurse who violates any provision of this Act;

(6) require a course of remediation, as approved by the Board, which may include:

(a) therapy or treatment;

(b) retraining; or,

(c) reexamination at the discretion of and in a manner prescribed by the Board.

(7) require a period of probation;

(8) limit licensure per terms of limitation provisions as outlined in Section 23 of this Act;

(9) enjoin or request injunctive relief; or,

(10) issue a cease and desist order pursuant to the provisions of this Act.

(B) Nothing in this subchapter shall preclude prosecution for a criminal violation of this Act regardless of whether the same violation has been or is subject to one or more of the disciplinary actions provided under this Act. Criminal prosecution may proceed prior to, during or subsequent to administrative enforcement actions.

SEC. 22. VOLUNTARY SURRENDER OF LICENSE

(A) Any nurse who is the subject of an investigation into, or a pending proceeding involving allegations of misconduct may voluntarily surrender his or her license to practice nursing by delivering to the Board an affidavit stating that the nurse desires to surrender the license or privilege and that the action is freely and voluntarily taken, and not the result of duress or coercion.

(B) Upon receipt of the required affidavit, the Board shall enter an order revoking or suspending the license of the nurse.

(C) The voluntary surrender of a license shall not preclude the imposition of criminal or civil penalties and fines against the licensee.

SEC. 23. VOLUNTARY LIMITATION OR SURRENDER OF LICENSE BY IMPAIRED NURSE

(A)(1) Any license issued under this Act may be voluntarily limited by the licensee either:

(a) permanently;

(b) for an indefinite period of time to be restored at the discretion of the Board; or,

(c) for a definite period of time under an agreement between the licensee and the Board.

(2) During the period of time the license has been limited, the licensee shall not engage in the practice or activities which are the subject of the voluntary limitation of practice.

(3) The Board, through regulation, shall determine general standards for structuring limited practice arrangements.

(B) Any individual who voluntarily surrenders his or her license under sections 22 or 23 of this Act shall not practice, attempt to practice or offer to practice nursing and shall be considered unlicensed. The Board shall determine, through regulation, reasonable annual fees for retaining records and ensuring compliance with the provisions for voluntary surrender of license, if the surrender is not permanent.

SUBCHAPTER V. HEARINGS; JUDICIAL AND ADMINISTRATIVE REVIEW

SEC. 24. HEARINGS

(A) Before the Board initiates formal disciplinary action, it shall give the individual against whom the action is contemplated an opportunity for a hearing.

(B) The Board, at its discretion, may request the applicant or licensee to attend a settlement conference prior to holding a hearing under this section, and may enter into negotiated settlement agreements and consent decrees to carry out its functions.

(C)(1) Except to the extent that this Act specifically provides otherwise, the Board shall give notice and shall conduct the formal hearing in accordance with the State Administrative Procedures Act **[citation needed]**.

(2) If the Board determines injunctive relief is appropriate, the Board may submit appropriate pleadings requesting injunctive relief, or, alternatively, if state law provides **[citation**

needed], the Board may issue an order enjoining the activity, pursuant to Section 36 of this Act.

(3) In any prosecution brought under this Act, any person claiming an exemption from licensing under this Act shall have the burden of proving entitlement to exemption.

(D) The hearing notice to be given to the individual shall be sent by certified mail to the last known address of the individual at least fifteen days before the hearing.

(E) The individual may be represented at the hearing by counsel.

(F)(1) The Board may administer oaths and require the attendance and testimony of witnesses and the production of books, papers and other evidence in connection with any proceeding under this section.

(2) The Board shall require the attendance of witnesses and the production of books, papers and other evidence reasonably requested by the person against whom an action is contemplated.

(3) In case of contumacy by the person against whom action is contemplated or refusal to obey a subpoena issued by the Board, a Board may refer the matter to state court, which may by order require the person to appear and give testimony or produce books, papers or other evidence bearing on the hearing. Refusal to obey such an order shall constitute contempt of court.

(G) If, after due notice, the individual against whom the action is contemplated fails or refuses to appear, a Board may nevertheless hear and determine the matter.

(H) A Board shall issue its decision in writing within ___ days after conducting a hearing.

SEC. 25. PHYSICAL AND MENTAL EXAMINATIONS

(A) The Board may require a nurse to submit to a mental or physical examination whenever it has probable cause to believe that a nurse is in violation of subsections (A)(5) and (6) of Section 19 of this Act. The examination shall be conducted by one or more health care professionals designated by the Board, who shall report the findings considering the nature and extent of the impairment, if any, to the Board and to the health care professional who was examined.

(B) Notwithstanding the findings of the examination commissioned by the Board, the nurse may submit, in any proceedings before the Board or other adjudicatory body, the findings of an examination conducted by one or more health care professionals of his or her choice to rebut the findings of the examination commissioned by the Board.

(C) Willful failure or refusal to submit to an examination requested by the Board shall be considered affirmative evidence that the nurse is in violation of subsection (A)(5) and (6) of Section 19 and the nurse then shall not be entitled to submit the findings of any other examination in disciplinary or adjudicatory proceedings related to this violation.

SUBCHAPTER VI. OTHER REMEDIES

SEC. 26. SUMMARY ACTION

(A) If the Board determines, after investigation, that the conduct of a licensee or unlicensed individual acting or representing himself or herself as a nurse presents an imminent danger to the health and safety of the residents of this State, the Board may, without first holding a hearing, summarily suspend or restrict his or her license to practice nursing or any unlicensed activity consistent with practicing nursing.

(B) The Board, at the time of the summary suspension or restriction of a license, shall provide the licensee with written notice stating the action that is being taken, the basis for the action and the right of the licensee or unlicensed individual to request a hearing.

(C) The licensee or unlicensed individual shall have the right to request a hearing within 72 hours after service of notice of the action taken by the Board. The State or Board shall hold a hearing within 72 hours of receipt of a timely request, and shall issue a decision within 72 hours after the hearing.

(D) Every decision and order adverse to a licensee or unlicensed individual shall be in writing and shall be accompanied by findings of fact and conclusion of law. The findings shall be supported by, and in accordance with, reliable, probative and substantial evidence. The State or the Board shall provide a copy of the decision and order and accompanying findings of fact and conclusion of law to each party to a case or his or her attorney of record.

(E) Any person aggrieved by a final summary action may file an appeal in accordance with the state Administrative Procedures Act **[title and citation needed]**.

Sec. 27. Cease and desist orders

(A) When the Board or the State, after investigation but prior to a hearing, has cause to believe that any person is violating any provision of this Act and the violation has caused or may cause immediate and irreparable harm to the public, the Board or the State may issue an order requiring the alleged violator to cease and desist immediately from the violation. The order shall be served by certified mail or delivery in person.

(B)(1) The alleged violator may, within 15 days of the service of an order, submit a written request to the Board or the State to hold a hearing on the alleged violation

(2) Upon receipt of a timely request, the Board or the State shall conduct a hearing and render a decision pursuant to the provisions of the state Administrative Procedures Act **[citation needed]**.

(C)(1) The alleged violator may, within ___ days of the service of an order, submit a written request to the Board or the State for an expedited hearing on the alleged violation, in which case he or she shall waive his or her right to the ___-day notice required by this Act.

(2) Upon receipt of a timely request for an expedited hearing, the Board or the State shall conduct a hearing within ___ days of the date of receiving the request and shall deliver a written notice of the hearing to the alleged violator, at his or her last known address, by any means guaranteed to be received at least ___ days before the hearing date.

(3) The Board or the State shall issue a decision within ___ days after an expedited hearing.

(D) If a request for a hearing is not made, the order of the Board or the State to cease and desist is final.

(E) If, after a hearing, the Board or the State determines that the alleged violator is not in violation of this Act, the Board shall revoke the order to cease and desist.

(F) If any person fails to comply with a lawful order of a Board or the State issued pursuant to this section, the Board or the State may petition the court to issue an order compelling compliance or take any other action authorized by this Act.

SUBCHAPTER VII. REINSTATEMENT OF SUSPENDED, REVOKED LICENSE; RE-ESTABLISHMENT OF FULL LICENSURE

SEC. 28. REINSTATEMENT

(A) Except as provided in this Act, the Board may reinstate the license of the individual whose license has been suspended or revoked by the Board only in accordance with:

(1) the terms and conditions of the order of suspension or revocation; or,

(2) a final judgment or order in any proceeding for review.

(B)(1) If an order of suspension or revocation was based on conviction for a crime which bears directly on the fitness of the individual to be licensed, and the conviction is overturned at any stage of appeal or post-conviction proceedings, the suspension or revocation shall end when the conviction is overturned.

(2) After the process of review is completed, the clerk of the court issuing the final disposition of the case shall notify the Board of that disposition.

(C) Limited licenses shall be reinstated to full licenses after the nurse fulfills the conditions of the remediation as determined by the Board.

SUBCHAPTER VIII. TITLE PROTECTION

SEC. 29. USE OF TITLE

(A) A person licensed to practice nursing as a registered nurse in the State may use the titles and terms "nurse," "licensed professional nurse," "licensed nurse," "registered professional nurse," "registered nurse," and the abbreviation "RN."

(B) A person licensed to practice nursing as a licensed practical/vocational nurse in the State may use the titles and terms "nurse," "practical nurse," "vocational nurse" and the abbreviations "LPN," "LVN" and "LP/VN."

(C) A person authorized by the Board to practice nursing as an advanced practice registered nurse, may use the title "advanced practice registered nurse" and the abbreviation "APRN."

(D) A person authorized by the Board to practice nursing as an advanced practice registered nurse, may use specialty designations above and beyond the title and abbreviations authorized in paragraph (C) of this section as deemed appropriate by the Board and promulgated through regulation.

SEC. 30. REPRESENTATIONS PROHIBITED

Any person who inappropriately holds himself or herself out as a nurse, either through the use of titles and abbreviations authorized under Section 29 of this Act or through titles and abbreviations authorized through Board regulation, may be enjoined from further practice for the misrepresentation, and fined and sanctioned under this Act or the state consumer protection laws **[title and citation needed]** or other applicable state statutes.

SUBCHAPTER IX. RELATED PROVISIONS

SEC. 31. DETERMINATION OF DEATH BY A REGISTERED NURSE

(A) A nurse licensed under this Act may make a determination and pronouncement of death under the following instances:

(1) The nurse has obtained certification as an advanced practice registered nurse and is the attending health care professional of record, or

(2) The nurse is a registered professional nurse and the attending health care professional has documented in the person's medical or clinical record that the person's death is anticipated due to illness, infirmity or disease. This prognosis is valid for purposes of this section for not more than 180 days from the date of documentation.

(B) The Department of Health and Social Services **[or appropriate departmental description]**, with review and approval of the Board, may adopt regulations to implement this section.

SUBCHAPTER X. MISCELLANEOUS PROVISIONS

SEC. 32. WAIVER OF REQUIREMENTS; GRANDPARENTING

(A) The Board shall waive the educational requirements of licensure for any nurse in good standing who submits application for renewal prior to the expiration of the current license.

(B) For a period of two years following **[date of enactment of legislation]**, all references in this Act to baccalaureate education requirements shall be waived for all registered nurses, who fulfill all other requirements for licensure and who are in good standing within and outside of this State, who apply for licensure as a registered nurse. The Board retains the right to review and determine fulfillment of all other conditions of eligibility, including review of the application to determine if endorsement or reciprocity conditions application shall be applied to licensure requests.

(C) After **[date of expiration of this provision]**, all the provisions of this Act shall be applicable to all registered nurse applicants.

(D) Licensees with inactive status under the previous Nurse Practice Act **[citation needed]** may transfer to active status under this Act by fulfilling requirements promulgated by the Board.

SEC. 33. MEMBERS OF THE BOARD

Any member of the Board abolished by this Act shall serve as member of the successor Board to which his or her functions are transferred until the expiration of his or her term or the appointment of his or her successor.

SEC. 34. ALTERNATIVE SANCTIONS

Civil fines, penalties and fees may be imposed as alternative sanctions for any infraction of this Act or any regulations issued under the authority of this Act, pursuant to state statutory authority transferring authority to the Board to levy fines **[citation needed]**.

SEC. 35. INJUNCTIONS

The State attorney general may bring an action in State Court of **[state]** on behalf of the State to enjoin the practice of any nurse or any individual illegally practicing nursing or any other action which is grounds for the imposition of a criminal penalty or disciplinary action under this subchapter.

SEC. 36. APPROPRIATIONS

In addition to any appropriations, all monies collected under this Act shall be dedicated to the regulation of nursing practice.

SEC. 37. FOREIGN-EDUCATED NURSES

The Board shall promulgate regulations establishing conditions and requirements of licensure for foreign-trained nurses or foreign nursing school graduates.

SEC. 38. SEVERABILITY

Should any section of this Act or any portion of any section be for any reason held to be unconstitutional, such decision shall not affect the viability of the remaining provisions of this Act.

SECTION-BY-SECTION ANALYSIS OF MODEL PRACTICE ACT

Subchapter I: Nursing; Definitions; Scope

Section 2. General definitions

Included in Section 2 is a definition of "advanced practice registered nurse" which is consistent with that provided by the ANA Blue Ribbon Panel on Credentialing in Advanced Practice (see footnote A, "Introduction," p. 5).

Instead of a draft Model Practice Act referring to "medical practice" and "physicians," the model makes references to the generic group of "health care professionals" or "health care occupations" which may affect nursing practice. This more contemporary reference is a reminder that the nurse interacts with other providers, some of whom have obtained some independence through licensure laws, and who may work directly with a registered nurse without physician intervention.

"Licensing authority" has been defined to ensure appropriate incorporation by reference when the state uses the Uniform Model Limited Liability Corporations Act to authorize appropriate organizations and groupings of health care professionals for the creation of limited liability and professional corporations.

"Nursing" is defined to include practice skills and certain cognitive skills associated with practical, registered and advanced practice nursing. Consistent with ANA policy, the Model Practice Act includes a definition of registered professional nursing that has a baccalaureate degree requirement. The ANA Model Practice Act also includes a definition of licensed practical/vocational nurse, thus expanding the act to cover *all* licensed nurses.

Section 3. Scope of Act

The "Scope of Act" section is included to articulate the breadth of authority granted to the Board of Nursing ("Board"). Typically, Boards focus solely on the regulation and licensure of nursing practice without addressing ancillary scope issues. This provision discusses the expansiveness of nursing practice and provides appropriate justification for the extension of the regulation of nursing practice outside contemporary boundaries. Many groups within a regulatory system have overlapping scopes and work functions.[F] To avoid fragmentation and assure appropriate, realistic parameters for practice, the Board is vested with the authority to review carefully any activities beyond the normal scope of nursing practice to determine if the expansion arises out of a natural evolution of practice or an inappropriate exception. Likewise, the Board is responsible for reviewing any infringements on nursing practice by other providers to determine if those activities fall within the scope of nursing practice or are a natural outgrowth of services appropriately provided under other health care licenses.
This provision also grants the Board clear statutory authority to regulate every aspect of nursing practice.

[F] Shimberg, B., and Roederer. 1994. Questions a legislator should ask. CLEAR.

Subchapter II: Establishment of Board of Nursing; Membership; Terms

Section 4. Establishment; duties

This section authorizes the creation of the Board and outlines its duties as a licensing authority. The ANA Model Practice Act does not include any recommendations of Board size. Also, the Act does not include any recommendations of number of consumer members. ANA believes that while consumers must be represented on Boards, they should not constitute a majority of the members.

States vary in the selection process. Some elect Board members, others authorize legislative nominations with professional organization participation. Some states' laws mandate that state nurses associations (SNAs) nominate nursing Board members. While ANA believes the latter process is preferable, statutorily mandated inclusion of organizations in the appointment process has been reviewed by a few state attorneys general and, in some instances, found an inappropriate delegation of the governor's authority to a nongovernmental entity. This provision, like all others, may be amended to limit the Board's participation in the nominations and appointments process. However, support and participation in the political process helps to insure continued SNA participation.

The duties of the Board are outlined in this section and include the basic functions of enforcing and implementing the practice act, adopting regulations to define the scope of each level of nursing practice, and authorizing the practice of advanced practice registered nurses. Primary functions also include the development of opinions, by the Board, related to nursing practice, examination, licensure, and renewal of the licenses of qualified applicants.

Optional language is included within the Model Practice Act to outline additional responsibilities such as developing and enforcing reasonable and uniform standards for delegation of nursing functions; developing and enforcing reasonable and uniform standards for all levels of nursing practice; issuing subpoenas, examining witnesses and administering oaths; investigating complaints of alleged violations of the Act; receiving and reviewing complaints of violations and regulations; conducting hearings and keeping records and minutes necessary to carry out Board functions; invoking, or requesting that the State invoke, disciplinary action against a licensee or an unauthorized person practicing nursing; and, determining nursing professional and related multidisciplinary group structure appropriate for independent nursing practice as professional or limited liability corporations.

These provisions are optional, in part, because they already are incorporated under the omnibus language enforcing the provisions of this Act (such as in Sec. 4(B)(1) of the Model Practice Act). However, since Board authority has been questioned when Board activity exceeds licensure and discipline functions, some states may require an additional listing of ancillary Board responsibilities, in which case the ANA Model Practice Act list is recommended.

The ANA Model Practice Act expands the authority of the BON beyond traditional norms for regulating practice. Instead of working from an established scope for each level of practice under the Act, the BON determines the appropriate level and scope of practice for each nursing provider and promulgates this through regulation.

Nursing continues to have problems legislating its scope of practice. The medical community questions and challenges any change in scope. Any attempt to develop scopes only through statute means a return to the issue of second licensure. While nurses usually understand the scope of nursing practice, there are differences in scopes from state to state. The ANA Model Practice Act defines an overall uniform scope for every aspect of nursing practice, and allow states to define the levels of practice in a manner consistent with education, clinical experience and professional certification. This allows the profession to define the scope of nursing within the context of practical, registered, and advanced nursing practice.

Alternative recommendation: If a SNA is unable to work collaboratively with the Board, it can include the overall scope of practice through a definition of nursing. Define the scopes for practical, registered, and advanced practice nurses (by specialty) in statute, and include a provision authorizing the BON to promulgate specific regulations to keep scopes current with professional standards of practice.

Included in this section is authority for the Board to determine nursing professional and related multidisciplinary group structures appropriate for independent nursing practice as professional or limited liability corporations. This is consistent with the inclusion of the definition of licensing authority under Sec. 2 and would provide an option to address the barrier imposed by present professional corporation business partnership and limited liability corporation statutes.

Alternative recommendation: Review the corporations/business partnership section of state code to determine if there are prohibitions or other limitations on nurses forming or participating in the development of multidisciplinary or professional corporations. Often, the only change necessary is the addition of "registered nurse" after the listing of "physicians, dentists and osteopaths" in the corporation/business partnerships of state code and/or the inclusion of a provision which reads: "Nothing within this section shall limit or prohibit registered nurses from establishing or participating in the establishment of professional or other corporations created to provide health care."

Section 5. Qualifications of members

The qualifications for members included in the Model Practice Act are those presently considered the standard for licensure boards. Members must be and remain residents of the state of Board appointment, and must have been engaged in nursing practice for at least a reasonable period of time. The ANA has taken no position on the appropriate time of licensure, since states can determine what will be best for the profession within their state. An optional "new nurse" provision has been included which offers a mechanism for Boards to include recent graduates from nursing school.

Alternative recommendation: Many state statutes list the types of nursing professionals to be included on the Board. As practice changes and specialties evolve, the retention of such lists in statute becomes outdated. If a state retains this type of language, it benefits nursing to have the composition requirements of the BON placed in regulation, not statute. Then, as changes in composition are required, those changes could be incorporated through regulation.

41

Also, subsection (C) addresses perceived conflict-of-interest issues when a nurse is active in his or her professional organization. All too often, professional organization service is looked upon as a conflict of interest by nurses. No other profession limits or circumscribes service of professional members like nursing. ANA believes that professional organization service provides a new and unique perspective on licensure issues. Since the nurse who is active within his or her professional organization does not have a pecuniary interest in the licensure process, ANA considers that nurse an appropriate candidate for Board appointment.

Subsection (D) includes consumer conflict-of-interest provisions, and prohibits service by consumers who are training to become health care professionals, and by those who own, operate or are employees of a business which has as its primary purpose the sale of goods or services to health care professionals or health care facilities.

Alternative recommendation: Since there is substantial rapid change in the health care industry, nursing needs alternatives which allow appointment of consumers sensitive to nursing's concerns. This may require exemptions to the conflict-of-interest provisions because many knowledgeable consumers are employed in the health care industry. Following the precedents set by state conflict-of-interest laws for politicians, the alternative offered allows the Board or governor to override requirements if the appointee (or member) discloses the conflict and agrees not to vote on any matter which provides a financial benefit. When Boards are considering items which may cause ethical or business conflicts for a Board member, that Board member should reveal those employment/ownership conflicts and allow the Board to make a determination if a conflict exists. If the Board deems that there is a conflict, the nurse member shall recuse himself/herself from formally participating in the Board's decision making process related to that issue.

Subsection (E) limits professional member conflict of interest by prohibiting the nurse from acting on his or her own application for license or license renewal or any matter related to his or her nursing practice, but it does not address nurse employment or ownership conflicts. Nurse members with ownership interest in health care concerns should consider revealing their interests and allowing the Board to determine if a conflict of interest exists, or recusing themselves from the process when acting on licenses of any employees of their businesses.

Section 6. Terms of members; filling of vacancies

This provision includes the length of the term of Board members, to be determined by each state, with a provision allowing for the selection of nurses for the Board for the first term of office under new legislation.

Subsection (D) allows for vacancies on the board to be filled in the same manner as the original appointment was made. Subsection (E) allows members to fill a vacancy only until the expiration of the term or until a successor is appointed and sworn into office.

Section 7. Limitation on consecutive terms

Though a provision has been included to limit terms, it does not include the number of terms to which members are limited. ANA believes it is appropriate for each state to make this determination.

Section 8. Removal

Section 8 includes provisions for the governor or the Board to remove members for incompetence, misconduct, conflict of interest, or neglect of duty after due notice and an opportunity for a hearing. Although the governor retains the authority to remove Board appointees, he or she may delegate this authority to the Board. Likewise, the Model Practice Act delegates to the Board the authority to define the standards for removal. If it is deemed appropriate under the state Administrative Procedures Act (APA), the governor may utilize a third alternative and transfer authority to the Board to conduct the hearing, with the Board rendering an opinion to recommend removal if appropriate.

Alternative recommendation: In those states where the governor has not transferred his or her authority to regulate licensure boards to a cabinet officer, work with the governor to obtain a transfer of gubernatorial authority over this function.

Subchapter III. Licensure of Registered Nurses

Section 9. License Required

Section 9 mandates a license to practice nursing.

Section 10. Exemptions

Paragraph 1 includes exemptions for individuals who administer treatment or provide advice in emergency situations.

Paragraph 2 includes the standard exemption for federal employees acting in their official capacity.

Paragraph 3 includes an exemption for nurses licensed in one state who are called into another state for professional consultation on behalf of a specific patient or to give a demonstration of a technique, act, or product at a clinic in the latter state, provided that nurse is in affiliation or has a relationship with a nurse licensed in the latter state.

Paragraph 4 includes a exemption for the nurse who travels with a patient to a specific destination, to ensure appropriate care of the patient during travel.

Paragraph 5 allows an appropriately licensed nurse from an adjoining state to practice in your state, if he or she is treating a patient within your state and does not have an office or appointed place to meet with the patient. The registered nurse pays a fee to the Board prior to practicing in your state, and the state where the visiting nurse is licensed allows nurses from your state to provide care in that state under similar conditions.

Paragraph 6 exempts student nurses presently enrolled in class or receiving a degree in nursing or enrolled in a postgraduate training program, participating in a course of instruction and under the supervision of a registered nurse who is qualified as a teacher of the practice of nursing. Other student nurse exemptions are for those working at a hospital, nursing home, or health care facility operated by the state or federal government or other facility considered appropriate by the school or college and in accordance with procedures established by the Board.

Although it is common for registered nurses to be licensed when they enter graduate programs, physician students are constantly expected to practice independently yet they are not licensed during clinical rotations or internship. This internal barrier to practice may well impede completion of a nurse's education, especially a nurse who matriculates through nursing and graduate school without leave or taking a break.

Paragraph 7 exempts only those who do not hold themselves out as nurses by title, description, or services. This is an expansion of a "typical" exemption provision found in many state practice acts. Though most provisions merely cover the use of a title or of holding oneself out as a nurse, the Model Practice Act contains added language to cover activities or services or "otherwise." This provision limits protection to those individuals who do not hold themselves out as nurses, or use titles and/or conduct activities considered nursing tasks. Paragraph 9 includes complementary language which sanctions inappropriate nursing activities. Sec. 20 includes additional sanctions for persons who provide nursing care and who are not licensed.

Paragraph 8 includes special exemptions for those individuals who are not necessarily carrying out nursing but whose activities may be considered a form of health care practice. These exemptions are applicable to members of the clergy or other religious practitioners and persons who are involved in the care or peaceful death of a friend or member of their family. It also applies to care by family, companions, or volunteers.

Paragraph 9 empowers the Board to initiate action against unlicensed persons who provide nursing care.

Alternative recommendations: To date, ANA has not developed a policy on the regulation of nurses providing advice electronically (i.e., "telemedicine," via telephone, computer, etc.). Paragraphs 3 or 5 of Section 10 may be used to regulate nursing telemedicine contacts. ANA recognizes the need to address this change in the practice of nursing and medicine.

Short of national licensure, there should be some form of registration of nurses practicing across state boundaries. In model legislation they developed, physicians are claiming that the electronic transfer of advice is a "medical act" which should be supervised by physicians. Nurses, especially those providing care in managed care settings, have provided advice and consultation electronically over the past ten years with no substantial problems. Working from practice guidelines or protocols, nurses continue to adhere to the common scope of nursing practice. For this reason, ANA believes that registration (the least stringent form of regulation) may be all that is required. (Sec. 3 clearly authorizes regulation of all aspects of nursing within the state and gives jurisdiction to the Board).

Until nursing establishes a policy related to nursing's role in telemedicine, ANA recommends the following guidelines:

• registration by all nurses, who practice outside the jurisdiction of their employment location. within all jurisdictions in which they practice electronically.

• inclusion in the registration of a waiver to claim jurisdiction outside the state(s) in which they practice, and acceptance to practice under the laws of the state(s) where the patient(s) reside(s).

• mandated reporting of employer(s) and electronic client base (not names, but states where patients are located); and,

• periodic review of the policy to ensure that it protects the patient(s) and provides the Board with adequate information to regulate practice.

Section 11. General qualifications of applicants

Section 11 includes the general qualifications for applicants as articulated in virtually every state statute. These include successful completion of a baccalaureate nursing program and no conviction for an offense directly related to one's fitness to be licensed. Also included are the educational requirements for nurses regulated under the Act and passage of an examination given by the Board as well as any other requirements established by the Board.

Alternative recommendation: ANA recognizes that some states will be unable to lobby successfully for master's education requirements for advanced practice nursing and recommends as an alternative that the state use language which will allow the BON to determine and promulgate additional criteria beyond the graduate education requirement for advanced practice registered nurses.

A second alternative recommendation is to have mandated "graduate" education for advanced practice. Presently, state Boards of Medicine (BOMs) do not include the specific requirements for specialty practice in statute but instead rely on professional certification. To retain consistency in health care occupation treatment, protect the ability of nursing to regulate nursing practice, and avoid barriers to nursing practice, additional authority to develop educational criteria for advanced practice registered nurses has been vested in the Board by the Model Practice Act.

Another alternative recommendation is language providing that, "The Board shall promulgate additional regulations to acknowledge certification of advanced practice registered nurses by any recognized member of the American Board of Nursing Specialties and/or by the American Nurses Credentialing Center.

This section includes nurse-midwives in the category of advanced practice registered nurses, although the American College of Nurse-Midwives (ACNM) has been reluctant to have nurse-midwives included in ANA models for regulation. The ACNM believes that midwifery is an independent discipline which should be a separate licensure category. However, many states regulate nurse-midwifery through nursing statutes, and all who are considered registered nurses are still accountable to the Board which ultimately licenses registered nursing practice. ANA considers all registered nurses with master's degrees in a clinical practice area of nursing or a related field advanced practice registered nurses, consistent with the ANA policy position articulated in *Nursing: A Social Policy Statement* (ANA 1995).

This section includes a baccalaureate degree requirement for registered nursing practice. Consistent with ANA policy, sections 14 and 32 outline flexible grandparenting and reciprocity requirements for existing licenses in good standing to assure that all presently licensed registered professional nurses retain the rights and privileges of licensure.

This section also includes master's education requirements for licensure of advanced practice registered nurses.

ANA realizes there are numerous boards which regulate RN and LP/VN practice. LP/VN educational levels are incorporated in this section, including provisions which allow the BON to establish the specific scope and level of practice for the nursing specialty.

Subsection (C) includes a provision to deny a license to anyone whose license to practice *any* health care profession has been suspended or revoked in another jurisdiction if the basis for the license suspension or revocation would have caused a similar result in another state, or if the applicant is the subject of a pending disciplinary action concerning his or her right to practice in another state.

Alternative recommendation: Since some states have statutes to cover different advanced practice nursing categories at different times, there may be inconsistencies in the statute beyond the definition. In lieu of changing the definition, organizations can work to define a scope which covers all APNs, develop uniform, consistent title protection language and standardize administrative processes and functions.

Another alternative is to ensure that all nursing functions are regulated through the BON, not the BOM.

Suggested Recommendation
Some states, such as Maine and North Dakota, have implemented a baccalaureate requirement for registered nurse licensees. Should your state desire to implement a baccalaureate requirement, it is our recommendation that language be incorporated into general qualifications section of your model practice act by using the following language:
> *"Registered nurses are required to have completed a baccalaureate degree, or its equivalent, in registered nursing at a school accredited nationally or with accreditation as determined appropriate by the Board."*

In addition, it is our recommendation that flexible grand-parenting provisions are incorporated into the statute. This will provide the flexibility necessary to ensure that all registered nurses presently licensed will retain continued authority to practice without conflict. Suggested language should read:
> *"For a period of two years following [date of enactment of legislation], all references in this Act to baccalaureate education requirements shall be waived for all registered nurses who fulfill all other requirements for licensure and who are in good standing within and outside this State, who apply for licensure as a registered nurse. The Board retains the right to review and determine fulfillment*

46

of all other conditions of eligibility, including review of the application to determine if endorsement or reciprocity conditions shall be applied to licensure requests. After [date of expiration of this provision], all the provisions of this Act shall be applicable to all registered nurse applicants. "

Section 12. Application for a license

Section 12 includes general administrative requirements for licensure, including the submission of an application and the payment of licensure fees.

Subsection (B) also lists fees the Board can establish for various activities under this Act, including fees for late charges, certification of advanced practice or other specialties, licensure by reciprocity or endorsement, and reactivation of inactive licenses and special charges for limited licensure status. The listing of the fees is optional in the Model Practice Act because it can be promulgated through rule making as well as being included in the statute.

Alternative recommendation: Many states are attempting to restructure licensure boards and remove statutory provisions that dedicate funds received by BONs to nursing licensure activities. This funding change limits the effectiveness of nurses in addressing licensure issues.

In addition to retaining dedicated funding language in statute, ANA recommends:

• inclusion of language in statute to give the Board absolute control over the funding of programs and activities related to the professional, discretionary functions of the BON, not to exceed the amount of funding obtained from nursing licensure permits, fees, and charges.

• retention through regulations, political process, or administrative procedure, of the right to review all books and records of financial disbursements, expenditures, or revenue received, based on nursing licensure permits and charges.

Section 13. Issuance of license (optional)

Section 13 includes standard language authorizing the issuance of a license which may be properly included in the regulations.

Section 14. Reciprocity and endorsement (optional)

Section 14 authorizes reciprocity when one is licensed in another state in good standing under the laws of the other state, and that other state has requirements substantially equivalent at the time of licensure to the state where the new request for licensure is being offered. In reality, few states utilize reciprocity because it limits Board discretion to review, question, or condition licensure based upon current but unproven allegations.

Section 14 also authorizes endorsement if the Board issues a license to an applicant who is currently licensed or certified and in good standing under the laws of another state, laws which, in the opinion of the Board, are comparable to the requirements of this Practice Act.

This section also includes a flexible endorsement provision to allow licensed registered nurses who may *not* be college baccalaureate graduates to obtain licensure under the flexible grandfather provisions of section 32 of this Act.

The ANA Model Practice Act authorizes licensure under either reciprocity or endorsement provisions to address issues of conflicting state statutes and licensure requirements and to allow the Board to acknowledge and provide licensure mobility without repeating the original licensing process. These provisions will enhance mobility because they allow for the use of either option and are designed to reduce the administrative paperwork associated with transferring a license to a state without a comparable statute. Likewise, these provisions were structured to enhance mobility and allow for transfer of advanced practice certification. These provisions are included as optional because licensure transfer is often included in the Board's administrative process.

Alternative recommendation: Though most states rely solely upon endorsement, if your state(s) can work with other state(s) to develop complementary statutes, you may want to include both provisions to allow use of reciprocity with complementary-statute state(s) and endorsement with others.

Alternative recommendation: Provisions also could be included which specify that, "The Board, in its discretion, may also accept the certification by any recognized agency of the American Board of Nursing Specialties and/or by the American Nurses Credentialing Center of any advanced practice registered nurse if there is compliance with subsection (a) of this section . . . ."

Section 15. Requirements for practice (optional)

Section 15 states that a nurse who fails to renew his or her license is considered unlicensed and subject to discipline and penalties if he or she continues to practice. The section requires the licensee to pay a fee for placement on inactive status.

Section 16. Reinstatement of expired, inactive licenses (optional)

This section authorizes reinstatement of expired, inactive licenses by paying the administrative fee, complying with the current requirements for license renewal and paying a second fee for reactivation and renewal of the license. Two fees are required--the first to address the cost of tracking and retaining records on inactive licenses, and the second to address the administrative costs of license reactivation. Sometimes the cost of both are merged into one fee. More often, Boards don't charge for inactive status but solely for license reactivation.

This provision prohibits license reinstatement if a nurse fails to apply for reinstatement of a lapsed or expired license within five years of its expiration. To become licensed after lapse or expiration of a valid license without being placed on inactive status, the individual must meet the requirements established by the Board and/or practice act for initial licensure. Again, this is an administrative provision which some states may choose to place in regulation or administrative code.

Section 17. Term and renewal of licenses (optional)

This section establishes the term for issuance and renewal of a license, with states determining the length. ANA recommends a period of not less than two years. This provision also gives the Board the option of changing the license period through regulation. This is another optional provision which may be included in regulation or administrative code.

Section 18. Continuing competency (optional)

This section authorizes the Board to establish continuing competency requirements. Recognizing the ongoing debate over the value of continuing education to assure competency, ANA uses the term continued competency to allow the Board to consider alternatives beyond traditional continuing education to ensure continued nurse competency. This provision is optional not only because it may be considered administrative, but also because some states have abolished or are considering abolishing continuing education requirements.

Subchapter IV. Revocation, Suspension, or Denial Of License or Privilege; Limitations on Licensure

Section 19. Disciplinary causes of action

This subchapter lists the causes of action for discipline. These were taken from existing statutes and are the types of causes of action most often listed by all states. Some have been restructured to allow specific causes of action for advanced practice activities. Others have been added or modified to address inappropriate delegations and infringements on nursing practice.

The causes of action listed in the bill include:
1. violations of any provision of this Act or regulations issued pursuant to this Act;
2. fraud or deception in obtaining or attempting to obtain or use a nursing license;
3. disciplinary action by a licensing or disciplinary authority or conviction or discipline by a court of any jurisdiction for conduct that would be grounds for disciplinary action under the Model Nurse Practice Act;
4. conviction in any jurisdiction of any crime involving moral turpitude, if the offense bears directly on the fitness of the registered nurse;
5. abuse of any narcotic or controlled substance and has not requested or is not receiving treatment for the drug addiction or abuse;
6. providing or attempting to provide, professional services while under the influence of alcohol or while using any narcotic or controlled substance or any other drug in excess of therapeutic amounts or without medical indication and has not requested or is not receiving treatment for drug addiction or abuse;
7. willfully making or filing a false report or record in the practice of nursing;
8. willfully failing to file or record any medical report as required by law, impeding or obstructing the filing or recording of the report, or inducing another to fail to file or record the report;

9. on proper request in accordance with law, failing to provide details of a patient's medical record to a health care provider or another health care professional licensed under state law;

10. willfully making a misrepresentation in treatment;

11. willfully practicing nursing with an unlicensed or unauthorized person or aiding an unlicensed or unauthorized person in the practice of nursing in a manner inconsistent with Board regulations;

12. knowingly delegating a nursing function, task, or responsibility to an unlicensed or unauthorized person, when the delegation involves substantial risk of harm to a patient or client;

13. submitting false statements to collect fees for which services are not provided or submitting statements to collect fees for services which are not a documented necessity;

14. violating state and federal laws regulating drugs, including inappropriate prescribing, dispensing or administering practices;

15. performing or offering or attempting to perform services beyond the scope of those authorized by this Act or regulations promulgated pursuant to this Act;

16. failing to report facts known regarding incompetent, unprofessional, unethical, or illegal practices of a health care professional or health care provider, unless the individual knows or reasonably believes that such facts have already been reported and disciplinary actions have been taken by the appropriate health care licensing board.

17. failing to pay a civil fine imposed by the Board, administrative officer, or court;

18. willfully breaching a statutory, common law, regulatory, or ethical requirement of confidentiality with respect to a person who is a patient or client of the registered nurse, unless ordered by the court;

19. discriminating against a patient or client based on race, gender, sexual preference or orientation, ethnicity, or disease state [illness] or in the provision of services;

20. performing professional services under unsanitary conditions;

21. engaging in sexual harassment of a colleague, patient, or client;

22. physically or verbally abusing a colleague, patient, or client;

23. failing to use sufficient knowledge, skills, or nursing judgment in the practice of nursing as defined by the level of licensure;

24. assuming duties and responsibilities--without sufficient preparation or for which competency has not been achieved or maintained--on repeated occasions;

25. exploiting the patient or client for financial gain or offering, giving, soliciting, or receiving fees for referral of a patient/client; and,

26. violating an order of the Board, or violating a consent decree or negotiated settlement entered into with the Board.

Paragraphs 17 through 26 are the additional provisions which are included in some state practice acts, but not all. They were included in the Model Practice Act after review by the ANA Congress on Nursing Practice. Moreover, the inclusion of these and other causes of action in such detail ensures that a nurse knows why he or she is being sanctioned. They provide clear direction on the types of activities the Board finds appropriate and inappropriate.

The listing of causes of action does not indicate any need to regulate or expand discipline of nursing practice. BONs remain vigilant in their review and processing of complaints made against nurses for alleged violations of the Nurse Practice Act. However, it is obvious from the annual disciplinary survey of the National Council of State Boards of Nursing that few registered nurses require reportable sanctioning. Instead, Boards use their authority to educate and rehabilitate nurses who may violate practice requirements. The specificity of this section is intended to complement these existing Board functions by providing nurses with clear notice of actionable offenses.

The ethical dimensions of nursing practice and professional life are of paramount importance to the profession. Throughout the country, BONs regularly examine their role in articulating and promoting the ethical conduct of nurses. The ANA *Code for Nurses with Interpretive Statements (Code for Nurses)* (ANA 1985), nursing's code of ethics, explicates the goals, ideals, and relevant ethical precepts of the profession. The *Code for Nurses* establishes a presumption about the essential values of the profession and direction for the development of ethical practice. The *Code* contains 11 overarching provisions, each of which is followed by interpretive statements that provide clarification and context. The *Code* is periodically revised to reflect the maturation of the profession, the changing realities of health care, and the profession's commitment to enduring ethical norms.

Several of the substantive issues addressed in the *Code for Nurses* receive attention within Section 19 ("Disciplinary Causes of Action") of the Model Practice Act. The correlation between these two documents highlights the importance of these norms to the integrity of individual nurses and the profession. Central tenets encompassed in both include safeguarding patients and the public from incompetent, unethical, and illegal practices; delivery of non-discriminatory care; truth-telling and non-deception; protection of health care information; accountability and responsibility for nursing judgments and actions; maintaining competence in nursing practice; and guarding against misrepresentation.

Periodically, SNAs have made inquiries to ANA staff about inclusion of the *Code*'s ethical norms in state nurse practice acts. While there is variation among state nurse practice acts, the majority do not reference the *Code of Nurses* or include it, though some do make general reference to the ethical conduct of nurses. There should be caution about specifically incorporating the *Code for Nurses* into the actual statute without further explanation or context for evaluation.

Alternative recommendation: Attention to the ethical dimensions of nursing practice through provisions of the Code for Nurses, *position statements, and policies would be dealt with more appropriately through regulations and state BON advisory opinions. Additionally, state BONs can refer to the ethical norms of the profession espoused in the* Code for Nurses *and related documents in disciplinary hearings and other forums.*

Many states automatically grant limited licensure status to persons with disabilities under disciplinary provisions within the practice act. ANA questions the policy of imposing limiting licensure based solely upon disability. Nursing requires the use of certain cognitive and physical skills based upon the work setting. Nurses can function as nurses without having unlimited range of motor functions and certain physical capabilities, if reasonable accommodations are available.
ANA believes licensure limitation should be utilized with caution. Because the Americans with Disabilities Act (ADA) was written to address work place issues, ANA is concerned about its application to the licensure process. ANA believes the ADA may prohibit testing and evaluating

"fitness" in situations where nurses fulfill all other requirements for licensure. Instead, ANA recommends a case-by-case review if any disabled or impaired nurse is reported to the Board to determine whether limited licensure is necessary or appropriate.

Section 20. Other unlawful acts

Subsection (A) was added to allow the Board to sanction persons who are not licensed to practice but who are providing nursing care in violation of the Act. These individuals may be sanctioned by the Board or the Board may make recommendations to the state attorney general to take action under the state nuisance and/or consumer protection laws.

Subsection (B) is fashioned after language included in District of Columbia Health-Care and Community Residence Facility, Hospice and Home Care Licensure Act of 1983, which prohibits discrimination against nurse-midwives and nurse practitioners in the privileging process. It has been expanded to cover many aspects of anti-competitive behavior and to incorporate by reference state antitrust acts. The District of Columbia Health-Care and Community Residence Facility, Hospice and Home Care Licensure Act of 1983, one of the oldest laws granting nurses protections against anti-competitive activity, has not been challenged in court as being over-expansive or exceeding the intended reach of other state antitrust provisions. Unlike state "any willing provider" laws, which prohibit health care providers and insurance companies from limiting reimbursement to nurses, this model language has been designed to address anti-competitive behavior against all classes of nurses regulated by the Act.

Section 21. Sanctions available

The sanctions listed include denial of a license, suspension or revocation of a license, suspension and revocation of the privilege to practice as an advanced practice nurse or the suspension or revocation of certain privileges associated with the practice of advanced practice nursing (i.e., prescribing), reprimand, civil fines, remediation course requirement, therapy or treatment, retraining, reexamination, a period of probation, injunctive relief, or cease and desist orders. Moreover, this provision does not limit or prohibit criminal prosecution. Also, a nurse may permanently or temporarily surrender his or her license voluntarily or compel the Board to go through a hearings process.

———

The sections of the Model Practice Act from this section onward address discipline and appeals of disciplinary actions and procedural matters which may be superseded by a state Administrative Procedures Act (APA). Prior to implementation of any of these sections through amendments or changes to the nurse practice act, please review the state's APA to determine the necessity of these provisions.

———

Section 22. Voluntary surrender of license (optional)

The voluntary surrender provisions authorize the Board to enter an order revoking or suspending the license of a nurse.

Section 23. Voluntary limitation or surrender of license by impaired registered nurse (optional)

The Board may extend a voluntary surrender permanently for an indefinite time, to be restored at the discretion of the Board or for a definite period of time under an agreement between the licensee and the Board, with the Board determining the general standards for the structure of a limited practice arrangement. The Board shall determine reasonable annual fees for the costs of retaining records and ensuring compliance with the provisions of the voluntary surrender, should the Board determine the surrender is not permanent.

Subchapter V. Hearings; Judicial and Administrative Review

Section 24. Hearings (optional)

Before the Board can initiate formal disciplinary action, it is required to give notice and to provide an opportunity for a hearing. This section sets out the process for conducting the hearing--to include the option to conduct a settlement conference prior to a hearing, to request injunctive relief if appropriate and necessary, to provide notice at least 15 days before a hearing, to administer oaths and require attendance and testimony of witnesses and the production of books, papers, and other evidence, to require the attendance of witnesses and production of evidence and, in cases of refusal to attend or obey a subpoena, allowing the Board to refer the matter to state court. This section also allows the Board to conduct a hearing even if the individual refuses to attend. It mandates the issuance of a decision in writing, with state Boards determining reasonable and appropriate time periods for preparation of the opinion.

Section 25. Physical and mental examinations (optional)

This provision allows the Board to require a registered nurse to submit to a mental and/or physical examination whenever there is probable cause to believe that a nurse is impaired. The examination is conducted by one or more health care professionals who shall report their findings to the Board. Alternatively, the registered nurse has the option to submit the findings of an alternative examination, if it is conducted by one or more health care professionals, to rebut the findings of the examination commissioned by the Board. Willful failure or refusal to submit to an examination requested by the Board shall be considered affirmative evidence that the registered nurse is unable to perform the essential functions of nursing as charged or alleged in paragraphs (A)(5) and(6) of Section 19.

Section 26. Summary action (optional)

This section sets out the legal option of initiating a summary action in the instance that a licensee or unlicensed person presents an imminent danger to the health and safety of the residents of the state, and allows the Board to summarily suspend or restrict the license of a nurse without first holding a hearing.

Section 27. Cease and desist orders (optional)

This section sets out the legal option of initiating a cause of action based on the threat of or actual immediate and irreparable harm to the public, and allows the Board to issue an order requiring the violator to cease and desist immediately.

Subchapter VII. Reinstatement of Suspended, Revoked License; Re-establishment of Full Licensure

Section 28. Reinstatement

This provision allows Board reinstatement of suspended or revoked licenses only in accordance with the terms and conditions of the order suspending or revoking the license, or a final order or judgment in any proceeding for review. This section also allows reinstatement of a license when based on conviction of a crime which bears directly on the fitness of the individual to be licensed if that conviction is overturned at any stage of appeal.

Subchapter VIII. Title Protection

Section 29. Use of title

These provisions protect the typical titles and abbreviations given to licensed practical nurses, registered nurses and advanced practice nurses, and allows the Board to promulgate regulations to protect and authorize the additional use of specialty titles and certifications as the Board deems appropriate. Consistent with 1993, 1994 and 1995 ANA House of Delegates reports which discuss at length the inappropriate, and often times deceptive, uses of the term "nurse," this provision specifically addresses misuse of this term.

Section 30. Representations prohibited

Section 30 expands upon Section 29 and prohibits the inappropriate use of titles and abbreviations by a person who inappropriately holds himself or herself out as a registered nurse, and provides sanctions for such action under this subchapter.

Subchapter IX. Related Provisions

Section 31. Determination of death by registered nurse

This provision allows APRNs and RNs to make determinations and pronouncements of death when the registered nurse has obtained certification as an advanced practice registered nurse and is the attending health care professional of record, or the registered nurse has in his or her possession the patient's medical or clinical record which documents the patient's anticipated death due to illness, infirmity, or disease (state law specifies the appropriate party responsible for this documentation.). This provision also authorizes the state department of health to adopt additional regulations to implement this section.

Alternative recommendation: If this type of provision is a priority in your state, check state law to determine whether nurses are prohibited from making declarations of death in any other section of the statute. If so, have that section amended in tandem with the amendments included in the nurse practice act. Alternatively, determine if the department of health wants additional authority to develop regulations.

The ANA Model Practice Act utilizes some of the better approaches to determination of death law. In those in which registered nurses have been given this authority, most state health departments regulate the process. However, nurses might not want the department to have this additional responsibility and the department itself may not want it. As judgments are made about the structure of the legislation, the SNA should consider the approach preferred by professional nursing.

Section 32. Waiver of requirements; grandparenting

This provision allows the Board to waive the educational requirements for licensure for any registered nurse in good standing who submits application for renewal prior to the expiration of the current license. This allows for the advanced practice nurse, who is presently authorized in the state but who has not fulfilled new educational requirements, to obtain advanced practice certification if the Board deems it appropriate.

Consistent with commitments made at the 1995 ANA House of Delegates, flexible grandparenting language is included to ensure that registered nurses who are licensed are not disenfranchised by the new baccalaureate degree requirements.

Alternative recommendations: While the grandparenting provisions address the immediate concerns of initial applicants, other concerns exist for existing licensees, particularly treatment of existing licensees who--through inadvertence such as illness, family emergencies, etc.--allow their licenses to lapse, or who move from a jurisdiction which does not require baccalaureate education for licensure to one that does. The Board or nursing community leadership should determine how these scenarios will be handled. Typically, mobility and license transfer issues are addressed through BON regulation which is used to interpret endorsement and reciprocity provisions contained in nurse practice acts. Thus, optional regulation language should:

  • cover the registered nurses whose licenses lapse for extraordinary circumstances--e.g., illness or death of spouse, significant other, child or immediate relation--to ensure those persons are allowed to retain license without obtaining baccalaureate education.

  • provide adequate notice to registered nurses whose licenses are about to lapse under less than extraordinary circumstances. Governments consider rule making notice adequate when the notice is transmitted:

- in an official government publication, and

- affected parties are given adequate time as required by statute to respond and comment on the issues discussed.

Given the limited circulation of notices which could explain BON treatment of issues surrounding the baccalaureate education requirement, SNAs should advocate or accept responsibility for conducting a public information campaign for registered nurses about changes in the educational requirements. The campaign should include sharing information with national nursing groups and publications and health care providers and companies as well as others, particularly, licensed registered nurses who may be interested in relocating to a state changing these requirements.

Section 33. Members of the Board

This provision allows members of the Board abolished by this Act to serve as members of the successor Board to which their functions are transferred until the expiration of their terms or the appointment of successors.

Section 34. Alternative sanctions (optional)

Where applicable, this provision authorizes the imposition of civil fines, penalties, and fees as alternative sanctions.

Section 35. Injunctions

Sec. 35 authorizes the use of injunctions by the state attorney general on behalf of the state to enjoin the practice of any registered nurse or any individual illegally practicing registered nursing or conducting any other action which is grounds for criminal penalty or disciplinary action under the Act.

Section 36. Appropriations

This provision authorizes the dedication of funding to the BON.

Section 37. Foreign-educated nurses

This provision authorizes the Board to establish conditions and requirements for the licensure of foreign-trained nurses or foreign nursing school graduates.

Section 38. Severability

This provision contains a general severability clause.

LEGISLATIVE ISSUES OF CONCERN
WHEN DRAFTING PRACTICE ACTS

1. REIMBURSEMENT

_____ Review state insurance code to determine whether "Any willing provider" or "Freedom of choice" reimbursement language has been included in the statute. If so, determine if the provisions require naming each health provider, or alternatively, listing the provider in regulations. If so, amend to include registered nurses as providers in statutes or regulation.

_____ State might have other language allowing a person to obtain reimbursement for the health care provider of his or her choice. Check with the state attorney general to determine whether opinion or case law would prohibit or limit a registered nurse from being considered a "willing provider" or "provider of choice." (Also, look for diagnostic limitations--e.g. prohibitions against nurses using _DSM-IV_ codes.)

_____ Mandated benefits statutes. These provisions also may be found in the insurance statutes. Check with the state attorney general to determine if nurses must be incorporated by reference as providers to ensure they can provide the mandated benefit (and obtain reimbursement) under statute. If not, also check with the insurance commissioner to determine if there are regulations to implement the statute and, if so, whether the regulations need amendment to include specific references to registered nurses. Please note: though this language is usually included in insurance statutes it may be a stand-alone provision in another section of the code related to hospital regulation or health care payments.

_____ Medicaid laws and regulations. Check state law to ensure that advanced practice registered nurses (APRNs) are named as providers.

_____ Hospital laws and regulations. Some states have statutes related to the regulation of hospitals or medical practice licensure laws which require physicians to serve as the primary provider of record and which merely allow nurses to collaborate or be supervised in the hospital setting, effectively diminishing the scope of nursing practice. Check to ensure that this type of provision is not in state law.

_____ As reimbursement does not relate to the regulation of nursing, these provisions should not be included in the nurse practice act, but, instead, in insurance codes, Medicaid, and other state statutes or regulations. Registered nursing should advocate direct reimbursement for nursing services. Also review Medicare statutes.

2. PRESCRIPTIVE AUTHORITY

_____ Include statutory references to appropriate provisions within the pharmacy law to ensure that limitations on prescriptive authority are removed.

_____ Include statutory references to controlled substances law to ensure that nurses are included as prescribers in controlled substances statute.

_____ Pharmacy law often has specific provisions related to the treatment of prescriptions of out-of-state health care providers. Review and amend to incorporate registered nurses as providers with reciprocity.

_____ Pharmacy law or state attorney general opinions often define the authority of the Board of Pharmacy (BOP) to regulate out-of-state pharmacies which provide mail-order drugs. Given the problems that advanced practice nurses have had with this type of pharmaceutical service, work with the BOP to ensure that the regulation of mail-order pharmacies includes provisions which prohibit anti-competitive behavior and provides statutory authority to challenge out-of-state pharmacies who refuse to acknowledge nurse prescriptive authority.

_____ Medicaid laws and regulations may provide for reimbursement of advanced practice nurses but they may not recognize advanced practice nurses as prescribers. Check the drug utilization review (DUR) provisions of the statute to ensure that nurses are recognized as prescribers under Medicaid, that their prescribing practices are tracked, and that nurses participate in DUR and the formulary development process.

_____ Check state attorneys general opinions on prescribing. These opinions may be clarified or discussed in the legislative history to avoid further attempts by non-nurses to limit the ability of nurses to prescribe.

_____ Sampling. Federal statute allows states to determine whether non-physician providers can request drug samples. Work with the BON to get the authority to obtain drug samples directly. If the BON chooses not to support this expansion of nursing practice, ANA suggests amendments to add language to the nurse practice act and pharmacy licensure and regulatory laws authorizing receipt and dispensing of drug samples by nurses.

3. DISPENSING/ADMINISTERING MEDICATIONS; DELEGATION

_____ Some states include language in social service or public health statutes, or the nurse practice act or medical practice act which creates a waiver of licensure laws to allow unlicensed personnel to dispense or administer medications in government-sponsored programs, demonstration projects or other situations. Usually, this provision is used as the basis for waiver of other nursing functions. (This may also be included in the department of human services or public health regulations.). Serious consideration should be given to advocating the repeal of these provisions. Alternatively, limit the use of provisions, which waive licensure laws to allow unlicensed personnel to conduct nursing functions, to specific sites under certain conditions, and mandate nursing supervision of the unlicensed personnel used under this waiver.

_____ Included in nurse practice act, social service statutes, or amendments to certificate-of-need statutes or regulation authorization for licensure of assistive personnel. Authority to provide unlicensed health care often includes the right to assist with basic "patient services" or "activities of daily living," including medication administration. Carefully review these provisions to determine if they infringe on licensed nursing functions.

_____ In many instances, nursing groups have opted to trade away the authority to dispense when pharmacists challenge nurse prescriptive authority legislation. Note that none of the states have repealed the authority of the physician to dispense and, in the managed care arena, nurses may well be called upon to provide this service also. Carefully review all provisions which prohibit or impede nurses' dispensing medication.

4. ACUITY RATIOS; QUALITY/SAFETY INITIATIVES

_____ Review hospital laws and regulations related to ratios. If acuity ratios are deemed necessary, it is better to place them in regulations than in statutes.

_____ SNAs are utilizing certificate-of-need laws to include ratios or quality criteria in statute. If incorporated for other licensed providers or health care settings, this is the best place for inclusion of ratios or quality initiatives in statutes.

_____ For additional support of acuity ratios/quality/safety initiatives, check out state or federal options short of legislation or regulation. Check with ANA's State Government Relations Department for options.

5. BUSINESS STRUCTURES

_____ Professional corporations. To ensure that nurses are able to create professional corporations (and provide services to health networks), check corporation laws to ascertain if your state has adopted the Uniform Limited Liability Corporations Act. If so, make sure nursing is included as the "licensed authority" to determine how professional corporations which include nurses should be structured. Also incorporate by reference (cite the state corporation laws in practice act and vice versa).

_____ Limited liability corporation. Some states are amending corporation and/or insurance laws to allow for the formation of limited liability corporations. Make sure your state laws have been structured: a) to allow nurses to be shareholders/partners and independent contractors (as opposed to employees); and, b) to allow nurses to form independent corporations and participate in multidisciplinary groups.

_____ State "Stark" anti-referral provisions. Although the federal statute does not name nurses as providers, many states do, thus limiting how a nurse may provide referrals. Review state law, and when in doubt, request additional review from the state BON and/or attorney general of these provisions and the limitations this law might impose on nursing practice.

_____ Medicare "safe harbor" regulations. Again, the law does not mention nurses, but it is intended to cover the activities of health care providers who are considered independent practitioners. Advanced practice nurses should check the regulations, once enacted, to ascertain if they are considered independent practitioners who should be covered under this statute.

_____ Managed care laws (HMO regulation). Laws have been enacted to address the structure of managed care organizations, as well as define the mechanisms for regulating the structure. Review these laws to discern if any limitations exist to include nurses among those not allowed to participate in the managed-care corporate structure. Also, because HMO laws contain pro-consumer rights and protections, the laws also often create job protections and benefits for health care professionals. The language in the managed care laws should prohibit discrimination and require due process for the removal of providers. If not, Boards should advocate inclusion of language which protects nurses in managed care settings.

6. INSURANCE

_____ Mandated malpractice insurance. Some states have mandated malpractice insurance requirements for advanced practice nurses. These tend to be placed in the nurse practice act but may be appropriately codified in the insurance code. Check both. These provisions are unnecessary and impede competition. Consider deletion from practice act or the insurance code.

_____ Insurance surcharge. Some medical malpractice insurance companies add surcharges for collaboration with APRNs without determining the actuarial base. Check with state insurance commissioner to determine underwriting process used in state and state laws governing fairness of the underwriting process.

_____ HMO regulation (managed care laws). Every state has statutes regulating HMOs and other managed care entities. Generally, these statutes are included under the insurance code and include anti-discrimination provisions which cover all insurance practice. Many HMO statutes include language addressing consumer rights and fairness. These may be used to address some barriers to competition in the managed care arena.

_____ Reporting of adverse incidents. In addition to the numerous federal and private agencies which receive reports, state insurance or licensure laws often mandate the reporting of adverse incidents to the department of insurance and/or BON. This information may come from a malpractice insurer, place of employment or federal reporting requirements (Medicare/Medicaid programs), state Medicaid fraud units, or the U.S. Department of Health and Human Service's (HHS's) National Practitioner Data Bank. Check state insurance laws and regulations to determine whether your state collects this information, and, if it does, if it reports to the BON. While you cannot control the reporting requirements, you may request, through regulation or statutes, limited disclosure of this information to the affected parties and the public.

7. AMERICANS WITH DISABILITIES ACT (ADA)

_____ The nurse practice act should be consistent with federal law on disabilities.

_____ Questions have arisen about the application of the ADA to the licensure process. Some BONs are developing a limited licensure classification for persons with disabilities that includes a listing of tasks, not education or skills, to define the ability of a person to practice nursing. ANA opposes this and contends it will not withstand legal review. If language of this nature is in your practice act, we recommend careful examination.

8. EDUCATIONAL CERTIFICATION REQUIREMENTS

_____ State law generally includes provisions authorizing certification of schools within the state. If this state certification is not enough, state boards should consider rule making related to certification.

_____ Because there is much inconsistency in the state educational certification process, the NCSBN is advocating development of a core competency examination to assess the knowledge base of advanced practice nurses. ANA urges states to move away from state certification to a national standard for the education of registered and advanced practice nurses and to retain the professional certification examination process.

9. INJUNCTIVE/ SUMMARY ACTION PROCESS

_____ State laws of civil procedure or the state administrative procedures act should transfer authority to the BON to enjoin or initiate summary action. If the BON does not have this authority, amend the state rules of civil procedure or incorporate by reference into statute the delegation of authority to BON

10. ANTITRUST LAWS; STATE WAIVERS

_____ Review state antitrust statutes, opinions interpreting the antitrust statutes, or waivers developed by the hospital association or medical society to facilitate development of managed care/integrated delivery systems. Make sure they are not structured to promote physician-dominated or physician-controlled organizations without providing comparable alternative corporate structures for nursing and other licensed health care providers. Likewise, check the HMO, MCO, PPO, and other managed-care regulatory laws to ensure discrimination is prohibited in the development and structure of the organizations, (Again, there is a need to review state insurance codes).

11. ADMINISTRATIVE PROCEDURES; APPELLATE PROCESSES

_____ The state administrative procedures act may outline the appropriate process for discipline, appeals, and sanctions. Should state law cover these processes, review sections 20, 21, 22, 23 and all of "Subchapter V. Hearings: Judicial and Administrative Review" and "Subchapter VI. Other Remedies" to discern whether changes are necessary in light of existing state law.

12. DRUG DIVERSION

_____ Is the drug diversion program in your state punitive or rehabilitative? Currently, nurse practice acts treat these programs as a combination of both without clear distinctions when the action taken by the Board is punitive. Given the ramifications of the Americans with Disabilities Act, the following should occur:

     a) clear separation of the administration of the diversion program from the BON regulatory function; and,

     b) inclusion of privacy protections by the *diversion program* to allow those receiving treatment to do so with anonymity.

13. MEDICAL PRACTICE ACT OVERLAP

_____ Most medical practice acts include language to allow the physician to delegate his or her functions to non-licensed personnel. Some physicians believe this alternative also allows them to delegate nursing functions. BON should request and carefully review complaints on inappropriate delegation by physicians, and articulate through advisory or other opinions the criteria for determining nursing practice and the inappropriate circumstances under which physicians delegate nursing tasks. If possible, nurses should review the medical practice act to request changes in statute to articulate differences in medical and nursing practice.

_____ Physicians' assistants (PAs) are regulated under either separate statute or the medical practice act and, in most states, they can supervise RN practice. Check appropriate law to determine whether PAs can supervise RN practice. If so, ANA recommends amendment of law.

_____ The medical practice act often includes authority to regulate specialty nursing practice and some RN functions (i.e. first assistants). In some instances, the Board of Medicine (BOM) may regulate independently, without collaboration with the BON. Review the statute to ascertain the amount and appropriateness of BOM control over nursing functions.

14. NAFTA AND GATT

_____ Review the reservations on licensure reported by the state BON to the U.S. Department of State to determine restrictions or licensure applicable to foreign nurses, including those entering the country under the General Agreement on Tariffs and Trade (GATT) and the North American Free Trade Agreement (NAFTA). Please note that existing provisions covering foreign-trained nurses cannot be expanded under the GATT requirements.

15. CIVIL INFRACTIONS

_____ Check state law to determine whether a provision exists for the assessment of civil fines, penalties, and sanctions. If not, the SNA should advocate addition of this provision or Section 34 should be removed.

16. PRIVILEGING

_____ The Model Practice Act includes privileging protections. Look at your state practice act and the medical practice act to determine whether limitations on privileging are incorporated into existing statutes. Some states have language either limiting the scope of nursing practice or creating barriers to clinical privileging.

Copyright © 1996 by the American Nurses Association. All rights reserved.

ENDNOTES

[1] Upon review of state law, ANA staff found some level of reimbursement but not a direct connection between the regulation of advanced practice and nurse reimbursement policies. For example, although California recognizes advanced practice through state law, the state does not recognize advanced practice through Medicaid statute or regulation. Private reimbursement laws only recognize psychiatric-mental health clinical nurse specialists (CNS) and nurse-midwives (CNM). Nurse practitioners are also regulated through statute; private insurers do not reimburse this practice. (Insurance companies may make exceptions to this practice, but reference is to the existence of mandated reimbursement laws, or an affirmative policy by state insurance companies to provide reimbursement to all NPs or CNSs.)

Alternatively, Colorado does not statutorily recognize advanced practice, yet it recognizes FNP, CRNA, PNP, NP, or NMW for Medicaid reimbursement and private reimbursement, effectively allowing all nurses in advanced practice to receive reimbursement. Licensed practical nurses (LPNs) and registered professional nurses (RPNs) are recognized under private reimbursement statutes. However, no states provide reimbursement at the 100-percent level. For example, Louisiana, Nebraska, and North Carolina have advanced practice recognition in statute or regulations, but no state reimbursement. Kentucky has advanced practice recognition in regulations, but state laws allow direct reimbursement at the option of the insurer. Hawaii does not have advanced practice recognition in law or regulations, but it has Medicaid pilot projects which allow reimbursement.

Though Illinois does not statutorily recognize advanced practice, a recent state attorney general opinion mandates that the state Medicaid program reimburse FNPs and PNPs.

In 1986, 13 states permitted direct payment for NP services and 17 states permitted direct payment to nurse-midwives. Today, over 29 states have direct payment laws which cover NP, CNS, NMW, and/or CRNA services.

[2] See South Carolina, Florida, South Dakota, and Virginia laws. Some states utilize BON/BOM/Board of Pharmacy (BOP) regulation. Some states limit the regulatory responsibilities of the joint entities. Others "invite comment" from the BOM (Maine, Idaho). Iowa law requires the BOM to "accept" rules adopted by the BON in consultation with the BOP. Although no cases have arisen from the use of this terminology, it is unclear how the state courts would interpret these mandates since these concepts and terms are not commonly used to explain the administrative law process.

[3] For example, Arizona defines a NP as, "a registered nurse who has been certified by the board and who by virtue of added knowledge and skill gained through an organized program of study and clinical experience has extended the limits of practice into specialty areas authorized by these rules and regulations . . . ."

Iowa defines an ARNP as, "a nurse with current active licensure as a registered nurse in Iowa who is prepared for advanced nursing practice by virtue of additional knowledge and skills gained through an organized post-basic program of nursing in a specialty area approved by the board. The advanced registered nurse practitioner is authorized by rule to practice advanced nursing or physician-delegated function on an interdisciplinary health team . . . ."

Minnesota defines a NP as, "a registered nurse who has graduated from a program of study designed to prepare a registered nurse for advanced practice as a nurse practitioner and who is certified through a national professional nursing organization."

Definitions may or may not include all the advanced practice areas presently recognized by ANA--i.e., nurse practitioner (NP), nurse-midwife (NMW), nurse anesthetist (NA), and clinical nurse specialist (CNS).

Some states have no definition of advanced practice, but, instead, list criteria for certification to conduct advanced nursing practice. Alternatively, some states also include advanced practice nursing within the definition of registered nursing practice.

[4] These states are Colorado, Connecticut, Delaware, Florida, Indiana, Kansas, Kentucky, Louisiana, Maryland, Minnesota, Missouri, Montana, Nevada, New Jersey, New Mexico, North Dakota, Ohio, Pennsylvania, Rhode Island, South Carolina, Texas, Utah, Virginia, and Wyoming.